Foreword

Throughout history people have been on the move from one place to another. In this way a large part of the world has become inhabited. For most of human history people moved in small groups, searching for new lands where they could live free from enemies and hunger.

The greatest migration, or movement, of people occurred between 1820 and 1930 and was made possible by the development of the railway and the steam ship. During that period millions of people made the long journey from Europe to America, but also to Australia and New Zealand, and from European Russia eastwards into Siberia. Smaller movements of people also took place in Asia, with Chinese moving into the lands and islands of Southeast Asia and Japanese out into the Pacific and to America.

Most people moved as a result of what can crudely be described as a mixture of "push" and "pull" factors. They were "pushed" out of their homes by poor living conditions, shortage of land, or lack of religious and political freedoms, and "pulled" or attracted to new lands and countries by the hope of a better way of life and new opportunities. For some people migration was largely involuntary: either they did not want to move or they had very little choice. Between 1520 and 1870 millions of Africans were forcibly taken across the Atlantic to America as slaves, and today there are millions of refugees in the world who have been compelled to leave their homes because of war, famine and disease.

Migration mixes people together, not only people from different parts of the same country but also peoples of different languages and cultures. Countries such as the United States and Brazil have been created by people from vastly different backgrounds. And if we look closely at the history of Britain we will see that our language and culture have been shaped by migrants coming to these islands during the last thousand years or more. Migration from Europe to the new lands after 1700 led to the spread of languages (English and Spanish to the Americas, for example), the development of new accents and new cultures, or ways of life.

The aim of this series of books is to look at different examples of "peoples on the move" – why did they leave their original homes? How did they travel? What did they take with them? What did they find in the new lands? How did they settle down? What were relations like between "natives" and newcomers? And what was the impact of new economic systems on the land?

If you have had the experience of moving home, perhaps from one country to another, or even from one place to another *within* a country, then you may be able to share the feelings of people who migrated in the past. If you have never moved home then perhaps these books will help you to understand the reasons why people move, and why in the world today there are, for example, people of European origin living in America and South Africa, and people of African and Asian origin living also in America and in Britain.

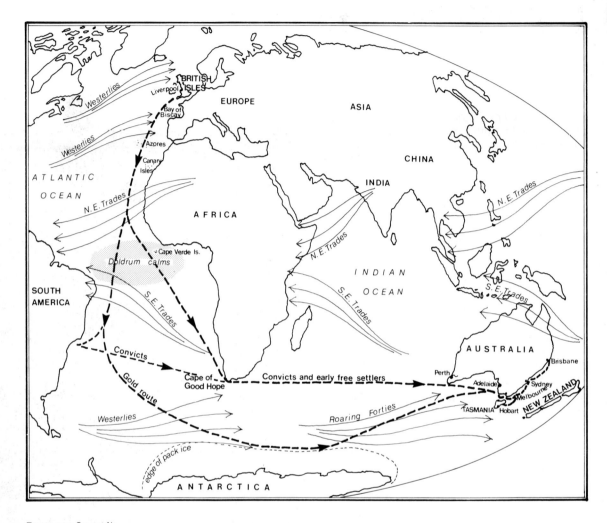

Routes to Australia.

1 A White Family's Travels

Since their first prolonged contact with the British in the eighteenth century, the Australian Aborigines have often been amazed, and disturbed, by the wandering habits of White people. Although familiar with lengthy journeys, Aborigines usually travelled only within familiar territories, whereas the British who migrated to Australia put vast oceans between themselves and the land of their birth, and often moved many times even after arriving. In many ways, Australians of European origin have been much more "nomadic" than the original native inhabitants.

The Aranda tribe of Aborigines living at Alice Springs in 1908 certainly thought this the case. They found the migratory habits of the White family in charge of the local telegraph station almost beyond their comprehension. Here was Mr Thomas Bradshaw, living a peaceful, well-fed life, preparing to take his wife and seven children away from the heart of Australia to the township of Adelaide, many days' journey south – never intending to return.

The Aborigines were especially worried about the future of the three youngest Bradshaw children, Donnell, Edna and Alan, who had been born at Alice Springs. They pleaded for the children's right to remain in their ancestral home, warning that it was wrong to leave one's place of birth for ever. But their pleas and warnings were in vain. Thomas Bradshaw loaded the buggy for the first stage of their 1500-kilometre journey. The other White settlers at Alice Springs gave the family a cheerful farewell party and then stood at their doors, waving. They shared the Bradshaws' excitement at the prospect of a new life in Adelaide. In contrast,

> . . . the natives came up from their camps and lined the road in mute salute, some standing sadly and with eyes only for the children, others sitting with their heads covered in tokens of mourning.

(Doris Bradshaw Blackwell and Douglas Lockwood, *Alice on the Line*, Rigby, Adelaide, 1973, p. 202)

Edna Bradshaw with Amelia, 1906.

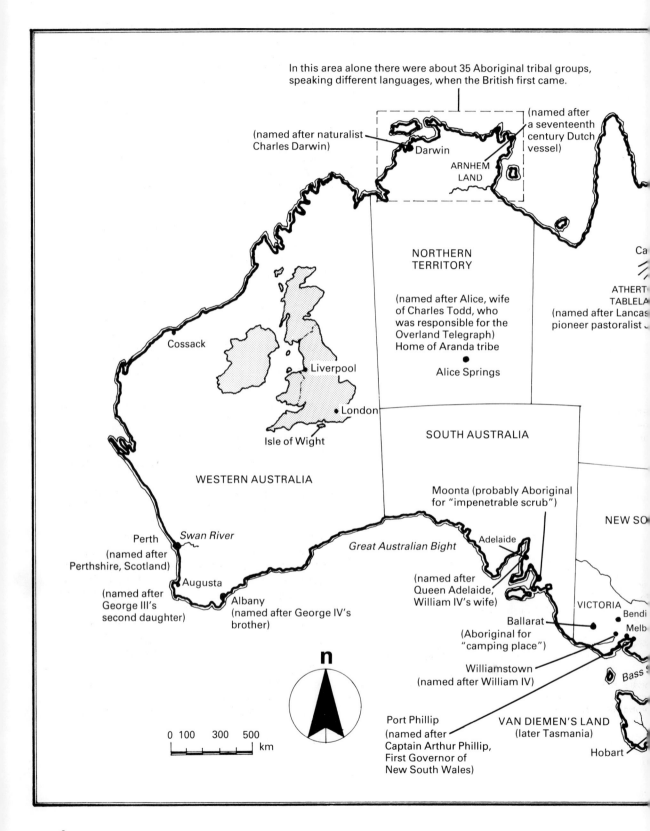

In this area alone there were about 35 Aboriginal tribal groups, speaking different languages, when the British first came.

(named after naturalist Charles Darwin)

(named after a seventeenth century Dutch vessel)

Darwin

ARNHEM LAND

NORTHERN TERRITORY

Ca

ATHERT TABLELA (named after Lancas pioneer pastoralist

(named after Alice, wife of Charles Todd, who was responsible for the Overland Telegraph) Home of Aranda tribe

Alice Springs

Cossack

Liverpool

London

Isle of Wight

SOUTH AUSTRALIA

WESTERN AUSTRALIA

Moonta (probably Aboriginal for "impenetrable scrub")

NEW SO

Adelaide

Perth (named after Perthshire, Scotland)

Swan River

Great Australian Bight

(named after Queen Adelaide, William IV's wife)

VICTORIA

Bendi

Melb

Augusta

Albany (named after George IV's brother)

Ballarat (Aboriginal for "camping place")

(named after George III's second daughter)

n

Williamstown (named after William IV)

Bass

0 100 300 500
km

VAN DIEMEN'S LAND (later Tasmania)

Port Phillip (named after Captain Arthur Phillip, First Governor of New South Wales)

Hobart

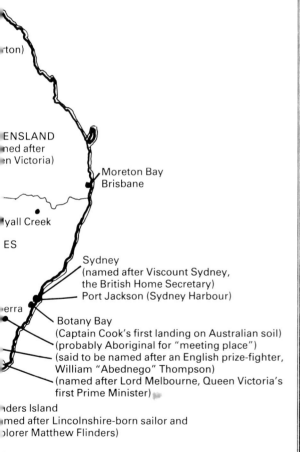

Map of Australia, showing the British Isles on the same scale and giving the origins of some of the place names mentioned in this book.

amed after Irish-born William Wellington Cairns, overnor of Queensland)

rton)

ENSLAND
ned after
en Victoria)

Moreton Bay
Brisbane

yall Creek

ES

Sydney
(named after Viscount Sydney,
the British Home Secretary)
Port Jackson (Sydney Harbour)

erra

Botany Bay
(Captain Cook's first landing on Australian soil)
(probably Aboriginal for "meeting place")
(said to be named after an English prize-fighter,
William "Abednego" Thompson)
(named after Lord Melbourne, Queen Victoria's
first Prime Minister)

ders Island
med after Lincolnshire-born sailor and
plorer Matthew Flinders)

glehawk Neck

rt Arthur and Point Puer

For Thomas Bradshaw, this was only one of several "migrations" he had made in his life. He had been born in England in 1859, sailing the 19,200 kilometres (about 12,500 miles) to Australia with his parents when he was still a child. His family settled in Victoria, but when he was 19 he moved west to Adelaide, South Australia. There he married Atalanta Hope Allchurch, so christened because she had been born on the liner *Atalanta* off the Cape of Good Hope on the way to Australia. In 1899, the couple set off with four children on the long journey north to Alice Springs, where Thomas was to be officer-in-charge of the telegraph station. This was an exciting job because the Overland Telegraph Line had recently connected Australia with the rest of the world. Before, the only contact had been by sea. But after spending nine years at Alice Springs they decided to move back to Adelaide because their children, who now numbered seven, needed formal schooling.

The Aborigines were sad that the Bradshaw family did not attach the same importance as they did to staying within a particular territory, but then these White people were still very new to Australia, even at the beginning of the twentieth century. The British had established their first permanent settlement as recently as 1788, and newcomers were still arriving. For almost 100 years, until the 1870s, new immigrants outnumbered the White people born in Australia.

Not all had come like Thomas Bradshaw's parents as free settlers. For the first 40 or so years the majority of immigrants were convicted criminals, sent to Australia to work out their sentences. But from the 1830s onwards free settlers arrived in ever-increasing numbers. Some left Britain because they found life there so hard that any change must be for the better. Others saw Australia as the land of opportunity and independence, offering room to fulfil ambitions and, especially after the discovery of gold, the chance to strike it rich. By 1830, people of British birth or ancestry outnumbered the Aboriginal population, and the impact of these newcomers on the land and ways of life was already making itself felt. This book tells a few of the many Aboriginal and White Australian stories of success and disappointment that form the background to modern Australia.

2 The First Australians

The Aborigines have been in Australia for at least 40,000 years, perhaps longer. It is exciting to think that in your lifetime important discoveries will almost certainly be made about the origins of these people who migrated from lands to the north.

The early Aborigines were hunters and gatherers, living in small communities in a sparsely populated land. There were at least 500 different tribal groups when the British arrived in 1788. The Gidjingali people of the north coast of Arnhem land, for example, spoke an entirely different language from the nearby Nakkara people. Most tribal groups lived on the coast, in the northern tropical forests, in the cooler woodlands of the south and east, and even in areas where, from time to time, it snowed. Only about 10 per cent of Aborigines lived in the inland deserts. Some groups living in the north were visited by fishermen and traders from Indonesia and Papua New Guinea, and so knew about people from "over the seas", unlike the Aborigines living on the island of Tasmania, to the south of mainland Australia, who had been isolated for thousands of years. Accounts of the first contacts between White people and Aborigines, some of which took place in the twentieth century, show that both groups were startled by, and were curious about, the unfamiliar peoples they faced.

A few early British arrivals realized that the Aborigines were well adapted to their environment and that Western values and customs were not always better than Aboriginal ways.

"Walkabout" was a word used by White settlers to describe Aborigines on the move, and incorrectly suggested rather aimless wanderings. The Aborigines travelled with a definite purpose. They moved as different foods came into season, and visited special sites important for their spiritual well-being. Where there was a good supply of fish, kangaroos, bogong moths, wichetty grubs, or millet seed, they might stay in the same area for weeks, even months. Some groups tended plants, but they were not agriculturalists in the European sense of looking after farms all year round. In the drier inland areas, groups sometimes camped only a few nights, collecting food on long journeys of 400 kilometres (250 miles) or more, carrying their spears, digging sticks, and perhaps even heavy grinding stones. The famous "returning" boomerangs were generally used for games rather than for hunting.

The natives of New South Wales, though in so rude [primitive] and uncivilized a state as not even to have made an attempt towards clothing themselves, notwithstanding that at times they evidently suffer from the cold and wet, are not without notions of sculpture. In the neighbourhood of Botany Bay and Port Jackson, the figures of animals, of shields, and weapons, and even of men, have been carved upon the rocks . . . That the arts of imitation and amusement, should thus in any degree precede those of necessity, seems to be an exception laid down by theory for the progress of invention. Had these men been exposed to a colder climate, they would doubtless have had clothes and houses, before they attempted to become sculptors . . .

[Perhaps] many of the accommodations of civilised life may be not more than counterbalanced by the artificial wants to which they give birth. But to clothe his body and to shelter himself completely from the cold and wet, and to put into the hands of men the means of procuring constant and abundant provision, must be to confer upon them benefits of the highest value and importance.

(*The Voyage of Governor Phillip to Botany Bay, Compiled from Authentic Papers*, London, 1789; facsimile reprint, Hutchinson, Melbourne, 1982, pp. 106-7 and 141)

Australia through British Eyes

The British artist Sydney Parkinson visited Australia in 1770 with the explorer Captain Cook. Back in London, Thomas Chambers turned Parkinson's paintings and drawings into engravings. The final engraving shows the Aborigines as Greek or Roman classical figures rather than as they really were: the paint and bone ornaments are accurate, but the Aborigines did not have wooden "swords" like the one shown here.

When the convict artist, Joseph Lycett, painted the Australian bush, he made it look like an English park. Although the long spear of the "blackboy" grass-tree and the emu on the left show the scene to be Australian, the trees bear little resemblance to the eucalyptus (gum) trees that grew there. These artists produced what they thought their British audiences would like, or understand, not what they actually saw. As historical evidence, these pictures tell us more about the attitudes, expectations, and artistic techniques of some British observers than they do about the Australian landscape and its inhabitants.

"Two of the Natives of New Holland Advancing to Combat", by Sydney Parkinson, 1784. (New Holland was an early name for Australia.)

"View of Lake George, New South Wales, from the North-East", by Joseph Lycett, about 1825.

Although some White newcomers were aware that the Aboriginal art might provide interesting insights into complex beliefs and ways of life, most were less thoughtful. The eighteenth-century British explorer, William Dampier, described the Aborigines as "the miserablest people in the world". Others agreed, dismissing the Aborigines as primitive people who had been "left behind" in the Stone Age, and who were physically and culturally inferior not only to "White" people, but also to other "coloured" peoples.

Aborigines believed (and many still believe) there was a very special link between people and their surroundings. A rocky outcrop, a waterhole, lightning flashes, or a lizard scuttling past might be part of an individual's spirit. Every Aborigine had a special place, plant, animal or event which linked him or her with the "Dreaming" or "Dreamtime", when the world was made. Beruke, a Kurung tribesman, had the kangaroo rat for his "totem", because one had run past his mother's shelter when he was being born. The special totems helped the Aborigines through life and warned them of dangers. It was important to the Aborigines that when they died, they should do so in their own country, so that their spirits might be at home.

Aborigines did not have the same ideas about land and property as the British. In general, the newcomers wanted well-built wooden, stone, or brick houses with several rooms, so that all members of the family could have some privacy, and also fences or hedges around their properties to separate them from their neighbours. They were often surprised to find that the Aborigines did not want to give up their rough bark shelters for more solidly built, permanent homes, and were quite frankly shocked when the Aborigines explained that they could not be bothered to keep such houses clean.

If the White settlers were shocked by the Aborigines' dwellings, the Aborigines were equally dismayed by White settlers' houses. The Aborigines considered that walls inside a house, doors which locked, and fences and hedges were bad because they divided people within the family and neighbour from neighbour. The Aborigines argued that White people carelessly built houses without any thought about the spirit world around them, and then spent far too much time cleaning their homes and worrying about them. The Aborigines explained that they would

Buludja, an Aboriginal woman of the Mungari tribe at Kwi an Gan (the Roper River at Elsey station, Northern Territory) compares the different ways in which Aboriginal and White children learn about the world around them.

That night, before "sun-sit-down", the boys and girls played on the edge of the water and the boys pretended they saw a Warbian [crocodile] which they were trying to kill . . . . It is during such games as these, when we are children, that we black people are taught many things which are useful to us when we grow up and which we must know in order to live in this land. What we learn from our play white children learn from books. The white people seem to have so many things they could do without. After all, the white ants eat the books, and people seem to find it very difficult to remember what was in them before they were destroyed.
(Quoted by H.E. Thoneman, *Tell the White Man. The Life Story of an Aboriginal Lubra*, Collins, Sydney, 1949, p. 34)

Crocodile painted on bark in the X-ray style by a member of the Gunwinggu tribe of Western Arnhem land. The artist has "looked inside" the crocodile, showing its muscles and digestive tract.

An Aboriginal family of New South Wales at an English settler's farm, by A. Earle, 1826. Note the White settler's "gifts" of tobacco, blankets, and a jacket.

not consider staying in a house where someone had just died, yet White people stayed in their houses generation after generation. So the White settlers who complained that the Aborigines were too lazy to build better houses were mistaken. A deeper reason was that White people's houses clashed with their own well-established way of life and their spiritual world.

Different values led to conflict between the first Australians and the newcomers, with the British being more determined to impose their ideas on the Aborigines rather than the other way round. The attempts of both the Aborigines and Whites to come to terms with different cultures is still going on today.

We have our rights and our customs which we obeyed until you white people tried to teach us they were wrong. Some of our people learned your ways, but mostly you only wanted our discipline and obedience. We lost our pride, which is very dear to us . . . . You value everything in terms of money but we place no value on it. Not many white men know anything of our sacred rites. When you are so ignorant of our ways, what right have you to say we have degenerated or are simple? We have often seen one of your people lost in the bush or on the plain and the hopeless mess they make when left to their own resources in this country . . . . There are many good customs, such as tracking and living off the land, that you have learned from us, but you asked to be taught these; we did not force them upon you.

(Buludja, an Aboriginal woman of the Mungari tribe in the Northern Territory, quoted by H.E. Thoneman in *Tell the White Man. The Life Story of an Aboriginal Lubra*, Sydney, 1949, pp. 128-130)

3 Those Who Were Forced to Move: The Convicts

Why did the British Government decide, at the end of the eighteenth century, to send convicts to Australia? The decision was linked with Britain's loss of her North American colonies. During the eighteenth century about 40,000 British criminals had been transported to North America, being set to work, virtually as slaves, on tobacco plantations. After the 13 colonies declared their independence in 1776, winning the war against Britain in 1783, the British authorities had to look for other destinations.

As a temporary measure, those sentenced to transportation were kept in old, unseaworthy ships moored in English rivers and bays. These "hulks" soon became very crowded, as did the ordinary gaols. West Africa, one of several sites considered for a new convict settlement, was rejected because of its unhealthy climate. New Holland, later to be renamed Australia, was also suggested. In 1770, the Yorkshire-born explorer Captain James Cook had taken possession of the east coast for Britain. He called this area New South Wales. Reasonably good reports of its climate, soil, and harbours soon reached Britain. In 1786 the Government decided that this was the most suitable destination for convicts sentenced to transportation.

Also, Britain stood to gain in trade and defence from having a convenient port in the South Seas. Trading ships and whalers would be able to call in for repairs and provisions, and some local products looked attractive to a sea-going nation, especially when wars threatened the usual sources of supply. Flax and timber growing on Norfolk Island, off the coast of New South Wales, might be useful for making sailcloth and ships' masts. The British Government also had to consider the possibility that some other power might establish settlements if Britain did not make a strong claim.

These commercial and political considerations reinforced the Government's choice. There were, though, no detailed, carefully thought-out plans for establishing a major port or trading centre. Although it is not fair to conclude, as some

historians have done, that Australia was founded "in a fit of absence of mind", the Government's arrangements were rather haphazard. Little attempt was made to select convicts and guards with special skills or farming experience and, in any case, the tools sent with the ships proved inadequate. If the Government's main aim had been to form a strong defence base in the Pacific it might have sent another expedition to find out more about the size and nature of the land – whether, for example, the east and west coasts were definitely part of the same continent. As it was, the British did not claim western Australia until more than 40 years had passed. Yet, whatever the Government's real motives behind the first settlement may have been, the distance from Britain to Australia certainly made it difficult to know exactly how to plan for the future.

Who were the convicts destined to make the long voyages to Australia over a period of 80 years, from 1787 to 1868? Were they harmless men, women, and children, victims of the agricultural and industrial changes taking place in Britain at the time, who were punished unduly harshly for stealing a loaf of bread or a pocket handkerchief? Were they hardened thieves and

---

CONVICT FACES

THOMAS GRIFFITHS WAINWRIGHT was transported for forgery in 1837. Well educated and a talented artist, he drew this self-portrait and wrote the words underneath. Convicts were often described as being full of "low cunning and revenge", but Wainwright was not serious in applying this description to himself, for he was a very sensitive man. Transportation almost broke his spirit. At first he worked on the roads in a chain gang, and later as a wardsman in a hospital He received a conditional pardon in 1846, shortly before he died.

MARY HAYDOCK, born in 1777, was still a child when she was sentenced to transportation for stealing a horse. She married a ship's officer, Thomas Reibey, and after his death made a fortune as a pioneer shopkeeper.

RICHARD PINCHES, alias Henry Singleton, had four previous convictions before he was transported in 1844 for stealing two shirts. He committed more crimes in Australia, and served over 40 years as a prisoner.

Photographs of convicts are very rare because the camera was not invented until the mid-nineteenth century, but in the 1870s a photographer went to Port Arthur to see a few prisoners still held there.

Head of a Convict, very characteristic of low cunning & a scounge!

murderers? Were they "political" prisoners, transported because they were thought to be a threat to their employers or to the British Government?

There were convicts in all these categories, and it would be misleading to speak of a "typical"

THOSE WHO WERE FORCED TO MOVE: THE CONVICTS

convict. On the other hand, many of those transported had similar histories. Many were unmarried men and women whose average age was 26 years. Until the 1820s, about a quarter were young people under 18 years old. Eight out of ten of all convicts were transported for some kind of larceny (theft) and had been repeatedly convicted. Although people were transported for stealing a loaf of bread or a pocket handkerchief, these offences were almost certainly the last of a string of crimes they had committed. Most were town dwellers, but may not have settled for long in any one place. They moved between the city and the country according to the season and availability of work, or opportunities for crime. Many convicts were poor, though this was not necessarily the case, especially if they had made money from their crimes. Nevertheless, they lacked security in whatever jobs they had. There were few opportunities to rise in society or escape from insanitary urban or rural slums. At the other end of the social scale, there were a number of "gentlemen" convicts, and a few

Leg irons, balls and chains, and manacles on display on HMS Success, *an emigrant ship which, in 1870, was turned into a floating convict museum. A complete set of chains for the ankles, wrists, and neck is on the right. The spiked collar went around the neck.*

women, too, accustomed to a very much more refined life.

About a quarter of the convicts were transported directly from Ireland. Many of these argued that they were "political" rather than "real" criminals, because English rule and very poor living conditions had driven them to desperation. Political prisoners from England included the Tolpuddle Martyrs, sentenced in 1834 for "seditious conspiracy". They had attempted to form a trade union in their Dorsetshire village when their wages had been cut to near starvation level.

Changes in English law influenced the numbers sent to Australia. The majority of convicts were transported after 1830, when, for

Caged prisoners on board a convict ship. In the worst managed ships some prisoners were allowed an area of only about 45 cm square (18 in. square) for sleeping.

many crimes, the sentence of transportation replaced the death penalty. There were relatively few convicts from Scotland, where transportation was generally reserved for those who had committed very serious offences. In Wales it seems likely that some women were transported to try to increase the numbers of women in Australia, and that men would not necessarily have been transported for the same crimes. Overall, though, more men were transported than women.

For some offenders the sentence of transportation came as a terrible shock. The thought of being exiled from one's family and friends in an unknown land was very painful, as expressed in this traditional Scottish ballad, "Caledonia":

> It was early one morning, before the break of day,
> There came a cruel turnkey [gaoler], who unto us did say,
> "Rise up, you seven convicts, I warn you one and a'
> It is today you sail away from Caledonia."

> We slowly rose, put on our clothes, our hearts were sad with grief,
> Our friends they came to see us off, could give us no relief;
> With heavy chains they bound us down, for fear we'd gang awa',
> Far from these bonnie hills and dales of Caledonia.

Others were relieved that their death sentence had been commuted to transportation, or had heard that it was indeed possible to make a fresh start in Australia. Many simply had no idea of the world to which they were going and could only hope it would be an improvement on their present condition. As Philip Moore, imprisoned in Aylesbury county goal for horse-stealing, explained:

> I know nothing of the place I am going to; most of us now under sentence for transportation would rather be transported than imprisoned here for hard labour for a term.
> (*Parliamentary Papers*, Vol. XXII, 5 February 1838)

The sentence of transportation: brutal or beneficial? It might offer a fresh start, and was certainly preferable to the death penalty.

Name: John Hudson
Age: nine years
Occupation: chimney sweeper
Where tried: Old Bailey, London
Crime: Breaking and entering the house of William Holdsworth at one o'clock in the morning and stealing one linen shirt, five silk stockings, one pistol, and two aprons.
Comment: John confessed to the crime, but the jury was asked to be lenient, since the boy might have entered the house only after the burglary had already been committed:

The only thing that fixes this boy with the robbery is the pistol found in the sink; that might not have been put there by the boy: his confession with respect to how it came there I do not think should be allowed, because it was made under fear; one would wish to snatch such a boy, if one possibly could, from destruction, for he will only return to the same kind of life which he has led before, and will be an instrument in the hands of very bad people, who make use of boys of that sort to rob houses.

Sentence: Guilty of breaking and entering, but not of burglary. Seven years. Transported on the First Fleet ship, *Friendship*.

Name: Mary Humphries, "Hellfire Moll"
Age: 30
Occupation: domestic servant
Where tried: Old Bailey, London
Crime: Highway robbery. Feloniously assaulting William Jones, "putting him in fear and danger of his life", and stealing his money.
Sentence: Death; commuted to transportation to Africa for fourteen years, which was replaced by transportation to Australia on the First Fleet ship, *Lady Penrhyn*.
(Taken from John Cobley, *Crimes of the First Fleet Convicts*, Angus and Robertson, Sydney, 1970, pp. 138; 141)

Philip Moore must have been disappointed to learn that prisoners were transported not only as a punishment, but also to be punished, and this involved hard labour. Work was also a practical necessity, especially for the early convicts, for they had to build towns and farms from scratch.

On Sunday, 13 May 1787, the 11 ships of the First Fleet set sail from Mother Bank, off the Isle of Wight. They carried over 300 sailors, guards, and a few of their dependants, and more than 700 convicts, together with 12 or so children who had been allowed to accompany their convicted mothers. There were four times as many male convicts as there were female. Their first Australian landfall came eight months later at Botany Bay. On 26 January 1788 the First Fleet moved a little further north to Sydney Cove, where there was a safe harbour and a fine stream of water. That evening the British flag was raised ashore. It has been celebrated ever since as the day on which European "civilization" in Australia began.

The colony's first Governor was Arthur Phillip, a former naval officer with some farming experience. His commission was read out at a ceremony at Sydney Cove on Thursday, 7 February 1788, so formally establishing the colony. The British Government in London instructed him to administer it with the help of a

Convict Sentences and Destinations
Between 1778 and 1868, 162,000 convicts arrived in Australia in 821 voyages. Half had been sentenced for seven years, a quarter for life, and many of the remainder for 14 years. The majority of convicts were sent to various sites in New South Wales, which included at first the entire eastern part of Australia, though areas gradually broke away to become separate colonies. The convict settlements included Hobart, on the island of Van Diemen's Land (renamed Tasmania in 1855), Moreton Bay (later part of Queensland), and Port Phillip District (later Victoria). Western Australia was founded in 1829 as a free colony, but from 1850 to 1868 convicts were sent there to help ease the labour shortage. South Australia, founded in 1836, was the only one of the six colonies never to have convicts.

civil and a criminal court, and naval and military officers. Civilians with special responsibilities included the Anglican chaplain, the surgeon, and the surveyor-general (whose concerns ranged from the first roads to exploration). Although Governor Phillip had to account to the British Government for everything he did, he had extensive powers and responsibilities, for it was recognized that it would take months, even years, for any query or protest to arrive from Britain. During the Proclamation ceremony, the convicts sat on the ground while the marine band played "God Save the King" in honour of George III, and Governor Phillip delivered a lecture on loyalty, peace, good order, and punishment. When some of the convicts tried to help themselves to food for a celebratory "feast", they were flogged, and one of them was left to grow hungry on a small island in Sydney Harbour, later appropriately named "Pinchgut".

There were no buildings at all when the First Fleet arrived. The Governor's first task was to have the convicts clear the land, build a hospital for the sick and storehouses for food supplies. The officers were issued with tents but the convicts had to construct their own shelters and, later, buildings for the whole community. The convicts found it tiring to work in the hot sun under the direction of disgruntled officers or fellow convicts who, because of the shortage of guards, had been appointed overseers. Also, they were disappointed that the Aboriginal population did not have wheels or strong metal tools they could use.

Governor Phillip had a difficult job, made worse by the failure of the first harvests and the shipwreck of two important supply vessels. By 1790, starvation threatened the colony. It was not until June of that year, when the Second Fleet arrived carrying provisions, that the settlers won the battle for survival. Even then, there were very few signs that this was to become a colony famous for its agricultural and pastoral industries. Gradually, however, a reasonably comfortable colonial life began to emerge. Government officials and well-to-do settlers entertained themselves at government receptions, dances, dinner parties, Sunday promenades in the park, picnics, horse-races, concerts and boating parties. On such occasions the contrast between their lives and those of the convicts was sharp; but at other times everyone shared the difficulties of pioneering life, which were aggravated by the length of time it took to receive letters,

instructions and supplies from Britain, and by natural disasters such as bushfires, floods and drought.

The rules for managing convicts in what was essentially a vast open prison were, at first, framed to fit each situation as it arose. Gradually an overall plan developed, which was extended or modified by successive governors and by the authorities back in Britain. Convicts were either chosen for government work or assigned (allocated) to free settlers as labourers or domestic servants. Violent and hardened criminals were sent to remote places of "secondary" punishment, such as Port Arthur in Van Diemen's Land (later called Tasmania). After 1834 boys were sent to "Point Puer", a special reformatory in Van Diemen's Land. Girls usually became domestic servants, working for settlers or for the Government.

Many convict women in government service were sent to the Female Factory at Parramatta, near Sydney. It was built as a temporary residence for those who had just landed, were on their way to work for officers or free settlers, or who could not find positions elsewhere. The women spun wool and washed clothes and, by 1822, wove blankets and rough linen. Both convict and free men were allowed to visit, and so the Female Factory also became a place where marriages were arranged and babies born. In the overcrowded building, quarrels and drunkenness were common. Women who committed crimes could be sentenced to solitary confinement within the factory. Female factories were also set up at Hobart and Launceston, Van Diemen's Land. Apart from establishing these institutions the Government also set convict women to such tasks as cleaning government huts, picking crops, and working in hospitals and orphanages.

Male convicts in government service were organized into groups of about 20 under an overseer, who was often a convict himself, and set to work on roads, bridges, public buildings, quarries, and public farms. As a punishment for laziness or bad behaviour they were kept in chains, sentenced to the treadmill, or flogged. Well-behaved government convicts were encouraged to earn money for themselves by working for free settlers in their spare time. This saved the Government some of the expense of looking after the convicts. Before convict barracks were built in Sydney in 1819, prisoners in town had to find their own rent for

a Trousers buttoned at the side, so that they could be removed without taking off the leg irons.

b String or rope to hold up the heavy chains, weighing up to 8 kilos (over 17 pounds) to stop them dragging along the ground.

c Leg irons, with leather cuffs to help prevent sores. The prisoners generally preferred to be called "government men", objecting to the rather derogatory term "convict".

d Life in the colonies was often difficult for the gaolers as well as for the gaoled. The shortage of men meant that the customary relief from organizing and supervising was impossible, but if this military guard left his post, he could be courtmartialled.

Hyde Park Barracks

These barracks, built to house about 600 convicts, were designed by Francis Greenway (1777-1837), who had been convicted of forgery but was later pardoned (freed) for outstanding service to colonial architecture. Over the years, rats living in the barracks made nests with cloth, paper and small items, which is one way, apart from reading documents, that historians have come to know how the convicts lived.

accommodation in private lodging houses. Most convicts went to live in the part of Sydney known as "The Rocks", where, according to some observers, they behaved as they had done in British slums, drinking, fighting, and stealing. Well-educated and skilled convicts were often given responsible government posts and had a good chance of having their sentences shortened.

Convicts allocated, or "assigned", to free settlers worked ten hours a day on weekdays and six hours on Saturdays in return for food, clothing and accommodation. In their spare time they could work for wages. The Government saw protection against revolt in having the criminal population scattered. Also, assignment relieved the Government from having to support all the convicts, gave free settlers much-needed labour, and was thought to reform criminals by introducing them to hard but useful work of the

An Assigned Convict's Letter

Some convicts wrote cheerful accounts of their new life, whatever their real circumstances, so that their relatives in Britain would not worry about them. They were also cautious about criticizing conditions for fear of additional punishment. Others wrote favourable accounts to encourage their relatives to come out and join them.

Henry Tingley was an assigned servant in Van Diemen's Land. His parents lived in Sussex, England.

Ansley, 15 June 1835

Dear Mother and Father,

This comes with my kind love to you, hoping to find you in good health as, thank God, it leaves me at present very comfortable indeed. I have a place at a farm-house, and have got a good master . . . . I works the same as I were at home; I have plenty to eat and drink, thank God for it. I am allowed two ounces* of tea, one pound of sugar, 12 pounds of meat, 10 pounds and a half of flour, two ounces of tobacco, the week; three pairs of shoes, two suits of clothes, four shirts, a year; that is the allowance from Government. All a man has got to do is keep a still tongue in his head, and do his master's duty, and then he is looked upon as if he were at home; but if he don't he may as well be hung at once, for they would take you to the magistrates and get 100 of lashes, and then get sent to a place called Port Arthur to work in irons for two or three years . . . . Dear Father and mother I have eight years to serve with my master, and then I shall have a ticket of relief [leave], that is to work for myself, and then to keep that for four years if no trouble, and to have my emancipation, that is to be a free man in this country . . . . Dear mother and father, I hope you do not fret about me, as I am doing well at present; thank God, I don't want for anything but to see you, my dears; so God bless you all for ever.

Henry Tingley

(Quoted in "Report from Select Committee on Transportation", *Parliamentary Papers*, Vol. XIX, 1837)

* 1 ounce = 28 grammes; 1 pound = 454 grammes.

kind they might take up when they were free. Assignment underwent many modifications but lasted for over 50 years until 1840-1.

Dangerous convicts, or those who continued to commit crimes after arrival in Australia, were sent for secondary (additional) punishment to Port Arthur, a special prison settlement, founded in 1830 on a desolate peninsula in Van Diemen's Land. Port Arthur convicts worked in chains, hauling wood and mining coal. They were flogged for any breach of discipline. The harsh life was a warning that rebellion or habitual crime would bring an even worse punishment than transportation itself had been. Port Arthur was designed to deter would-be offenders, rather than rehabilitate law-breakers. To prevent escape, soldiers with dogs formed a cordon across Eaglehawk Neck, a narrow strip of land connecting the peninsula to the rest of the island.

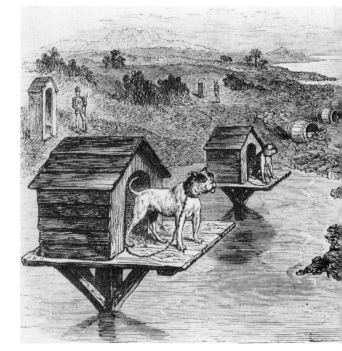

Cordon of dogs to help prevent escape from Port Arthur convict settlement.

THOSE WHO WERE FORCED TO MOVE: THE CONVICTS

The surrounding waters were shark-infested and the convicts were told that if they tried to escape the sharks would eat them or the dogs would tear them to pieces. Despite the warnings there were those who did try to escape – but few were successful. Many convicts were physically and mentally broken by these places of secondary punishment.

Many boys between the ages of 12 and 18 were transported, and at least one child was as young as eight. Fearing that the children would become hardened by associating with older criminals, the authorities eventually established a special settlement for them at Port Arthur, called Point Puer, "Puer" being the Latin word for "boy". The boys were sent straight there from Britain. An attempt was made to educate as well as punish them:

The Juvenile establishment at Point Puer was formed in January 1834 . . . . The whole of the boys are more or less taught the use of husbandry – tools, the axe, saw, etc. . . . The clothing furnished to the boys is the same as that allowed to other prisoners throughout the colony; viz. two jackets, two pairs of trousers, two pairs of boots, two striped cotton shirts, one cloth waistcoat, and a cap, annually. The bedding consists of one rug, one blanket, one bed-tick or hammock. As the barrack room is rather cold, I have taken it upon myself to issue an extra blanket to the boys who conduct themselves, but which is taken from them when sleeping in the cells, etc., or under punishment.

(Charles O'Hara Booth, Commandant Officer, Port Arthur, *Parliamentary Papers*, Vol. XXII, 1837-8, p. 220)

Most convicts gained their freedom only by working out their sentences. But some thousands were granted short-cuts to liberty. The Government introduced the short-cuts to save

"The Convict Tramway" by G.C. Mundy. A scene in the bush from the 1850s, during the last years of transportation to Van Diemen's Land. The convicts are being used as horse power, with the free settlers enjoying an easy 30-minute ride from Norfolk Bay to Port Arthur.

public money, encourage and reward good behaviour and, especially when labour was scarce, to persuade well-behaved or talented convicts to see Australia as their permanent home. Convicts granted either "tickets-of-leave" or "conditional pardons" had permission to work for themselves, so long as they stayed in the colonies for the length of their sentences. Only those like the Tolpuddle Martyrs who were granted "absolute pardons" on the grounds of miscarriage of justice, or those who had finished their sentences, were free to return to Britain. The Government did not pay the return journey. Some ex-convicts saved enough to pay the fare, or worked their passages on homeward-bound ships.

But the incentives to stay in Australia were fairly strong. Until the early 1820s, ex-convicts, or "emancipists" as they were popularly called, were given free land, tools, stock, and provisions to help them start life afresh as much-needed settlers. In some cases, free passages from Britain were granted to wives and young children. Even when less assistance was given, emancipists generally had more chance of finding employment in Australia than in Britain. But many wealthier free settlers, called "exclusives", did not think it was fair that emancipists should have as many rights as those who had never committed crimes. The disputes contributed to the social divisions of early colonial society. The differences of opinion were likely to remain so long as convicts were transported to Australia.

The supporters of convict transportation claimed that it was an appropriate form of retribution for crimes committed, an effective deterrent to would-be offenders, and an excellent way of reforming criminals – in addition to its contribution to Australia's growth. But there had always been some who had doubts about the humanity and effectiveness of this form of punishment, and by the late 1830s and 1840s transportation was under prolonged attack. One of the main problems was that the experiences of individuals differed so widely. Assigning convicts to settlers looked sensible on paper, but in practice, because so much depended on personalities and on economic conditions, it became a giant lottery. Assignment was not a satisfactory form of punishment when so much depended on chance. Probation was one of the systems tried in place of assignment. Prisoners had to work in convict gangs for at least a year before they were given probation passes,

allowing them to seek private employment. But this did not stop the debate that surrounded the whole subject of transportation both in Britain and Australia.

It was argued that since Britain had abolished slavery in 1833, the "slavery" of convict transportation should also be abolished. Also, it was considered less expensive to build new prisons in Britain than to continue sending prisoners abroad. Greater emphasis on separate confinement and other new methods of prison discipline were believed to be more effective than transportation. Improved economic conditions in Britain in the middle of the nineteenth century, including a heavy demand for labour on the new railways, and a change of government, also helped determine events. In 1852, the Whig Government was defeated and the Tories came to power with a greater willingness to consider the abolitionists' arguments.

Those who wanted transportation abolished also argued that it stunted Australia's growth because free settlers were reluctant to migrate to a prison, and the presence of convicts slowed down the development of political freedom. Developments in the colonies further strengthened the abolitionists' case. After the discovery of gold in the 1850s transportation was no longer such a deterrent. Indeed, in 1852, prisoners waiting in the hulks at Woolwich rioted in protest when they heard that their transportation sentences were not to be carried out.

The End of Transportation

Transportation to the colonies ended in the following years, although many convicts who were already in Australia at these dates had to finish their sentences there:

1840	**New South Wales,** including **Moreton Bay** (later Queensland) – although in 1849-50, 2000 more convicts arrived in a short-lived effort to revive transportation – and **Port Phillip Bay** (later Victoria)
1853	**Van Diemen's Land** (later Tasmania)
1868	**Western Australia** (convicts first introduced in 1850)

4 Those Who Chose to Move: the Free Settlers

Among the great beams, bulks, and ringbolts of the ship, and the emigrant-berths, and chests, and bundles . . . were crowded groups of people . . . from babies who had but a week or two of life behind them, to crooked old men and women . . . and from ploughmen bodily carrying out the soil of England on their boots, to smiths carrying samples of its soot and smoke on their skins; every age and occupation appeared to be crammed into the narrow compass of the 'tween decks.

(Charles Dickens, *David Copperfield*, first published 1849-50, O.U.P., 1981, p. 694)

Between 1788 and 1850 some 187,000 people chose to leave Britain and settle in Australia. What motivated so many to undertake such a long journey for an uncertain future? Those who could afford to pay their own passages, especially young gentlemen, saw emigration to the colonies as an appropriate "job", an alternative to, say, going into the army. Even when their knowledge of Australia was extremely vague they had high aspirations – perhaps to work for the Government, or on the land, and eventually to make enough money to live as "gentlemen of independent means" either in Australia or back in Britain. They arrived with letters of introduction recommending them to the Governor or other officials, for personal contact was an important way of finding a good position. The chance to own land in Australia was a great attraction, especially for British people who came from a society where social position and political power were usually linked to the ownership of property. In Australia it might be possible to make, or restore, the family name and fortune.

Others emigrated to Australia because they were finding life in Britain so difficult. Unemployment, low wages, poor housing conditions, cold winters, the fear of ending up destitute in a workhouse – all contributed to their anxiety. Changes associated with the agricultural and industrial "revolutions" in the late eighteenth and nineteenth centuries disturbed traditional

LOSING STRENGTH.

The great want of England is EMPLOYMENT; the great want of New South Wales is LABOUR. England has more mouths than food; New South Wales has more food than mouths. England would be the gainer by lopping off one of her superfluous millions; New South Wales would be the gainer by their being planted upon her ample plains.

(*The Emigrants' Guide to New South Wales, Van Diemen's Land Etc.*, London, 1832, p. 11)

patterns of life. Although some people benefited, others – such as the Scottish crofters forcibly evicted from small agricultural holdings to make way for large-scale grazing – were ruined.

Emigrants on the St Vincent *in 1844.* The London Illustrated News *reported on 13 April: "We witnessed the emigrants taking their first meal on board (good mutton, beef, potatoes and soup)". This picture shows the steerage accommodation for families. The bunks are at the sides. People slept with their feet pointing towards the centre of the ship, hanging their hats and cloaks on pegs at the end of the bunks. Apart from a few curtains, there was very little privacy. Children sometimes shared their parents' bunks, but on this particular ship they have their own. Light is coming in through an uncovered hatch, which would have to be lashed down during storms. A wide table runs down the centre.*

Distress reached a particularly high level in Ireland during the 1840s, when disease destroyed the potato crop, causing widespread famine. Some workhouse paupers were given financial help to emigrate, but, in general, the poorest of the poor could not do very much about their plight. But there were others, just a little better off, who could think about making a change. They attended local meetings held by clergy, landowners, and such groups as the Highland and Islands Emigration Society, who told them about the advantages, and some of the problems, of migrating, and how to apply for money that might be available to assist them with their sea-passages.

Migration was a "push-pull" process, well described by two Scotsmen writing in 1841. Some migrants responded more to the "push" noted by David McLaren: migration is "the means of deliverance from our native land . . . a refuge". Others felt the "pull" of Australia, as temptingly depicted by a correspondent to the *Dundee Advertiser*: "Our wealthy landowners riot in luxury . . . . There is encouragement for you all."

Surprisingly, those who sailed to Australia as free, that is, non-convict, immigrants had less chance of surviving the voyage than did those who sailed as convicts. On paper, at least, convict transportation regulations excluded the weak and sick, and some attempt was made to supervise the prisoners' diet. While it is important not to underestimate the rough treatment the convicts received, or to forget such terrible voyages as that of the Second Fleet when one quarter of the 1000 prisoners died, convict deaths through illness at sea averaged less than four per voyage. On the early, poorly supervised emigrant ships, the losses were often five times this number, especially among the steerage passengers.

Hamilton Collins Semphill was one of many who exploited emigration for his own financial gain. He filled *The Warrior* bound for Swan River, Western Australia, full to overflowing. Semphill also kept cattle on deck, instead of in the hold, which he filled with extra cargo, and animal matter oozed through the deck into the berths. A letter of complaint dated 3 October 1829 reported:

The whole of the Steerage is literally Choked with Berths and nearly dark. Poor men who

have paid from 25 to 30 pounds for their passages cannot find their berth but with a lighted candle. [Semphill's] avarice has been so great that he has not left a Table, or a space, for the steerage passengers to take their scanty allowance of food, but they are compelled to take it on their knees, their chests, or on the Ground . . . . I am certain that His Majesty's Government would not have allowed a ship of convicts to be sent out in like manner.

(Quoted in J.M.R. Cameron, *Ambition's Fire, The Agricultural Colonization of Pre-Convict Western Australia*, University of Western Australia, 1981, p. 83)

As well as diseases and fire on board, the dangers of the sea routes claimed many lives. Over 500 convicts lost their lives in shipwrecks, but probably as many as 2500 free emigrants drowned. This is partly explained by the greater number of emigrants who set out, and partly by the more dangerous, though potentially faster, routes taken by many emigrant "clipper" ships. In the 1850s the old route to Australia by way of the

Cape of Good Hope, Africa, returning to Britain round Cape Horn, South America, was modified. Now clipper ships sailed nearer Antarctica, to take advantage of the strong Roaring Forties and Fifties winds. Mountainous waves towered above the ships and drifting icebergs became deadly traps. In the southern summer of 1854-5 an emigrant ship, *The Guiding Star*, with 546 people on board, sailed into a huge horseshoe-shaped island of ice and did not sail out again.

The voyage to Australia, though, was less dangerous than the Atlantic route from Britain to North America, especially in the period before 1855. The shorter and cheaper Atlantic crossing tended to attract many people who were already sick and weak, such as the Irish fleeing in 1847 from the potato famine, who died in their thousands at sea from typhus. Laws regulating conditions on emigrant ships were generally more strictly enforced on ships bound for Australia because the voyage was longer. More important, once government authorities began to assist migrants with their fares to Australia in the 1830s and 1840s they gradually took more interest in safe arrivals.

In the first decades of Australian settlement, most free emigrants were reasonably well-to-do. Few labourers could afford the fare, which was often five or six times higher than that to North America. Therefore, free settlers depended heavily on convict and ex-convict labour. There had always been some who thought it was unwise to base Australia's development on convicts, but it was not until 1829 that anyone offered an acceptable alternative. In that year, Edward Gibbon Wakefield published a series of influential newspaper articles in Britain, proposing that colonial land should be sold, not given away, and that the money raised should be used to bring working-class immigrants to the colonies. The British Government welcomed a scheme that promised emigration for part of Britain's "surplus population" without expense to the Mother country. The colonies welcomed it because they had plenty of land which could be sold. Wakefield's articles were reprinted as *A Letter from Sydney* (even though he was very much in London, having been gaoled for abducting a schoolgirl heiress and forcing her to marry him at Gretna Green).

The formation of a new colony, South Australia, in 1836 was one of the main testing grounds for Wakefieldian ideas of "systematic colonization". It was founded as a free colony without the convict "taint" that marked most of its neighbours, and money from land sales was used to pay for migration. Although South Australia encountered many problems, including the misuse of land

"A Settlers First Hut" by A.D. Lang, 1842. The settler's sea-chests are now being used as tables. Although his hut may not be better than the one he left behind in Britain (a piece of sack covers the window and there is no ceiling), he is enjoying the independence of sitting in his own hut, with his hunting trophies, pipes, and other possessions around him.

funds, it was never forced to introduce convict labour.

In New South Wales, from 1832, some of the money from land sales was used to pay the passages of people who came to be called "assisted migrants". In 1835 this scheme was supplemented by a bounty system, whereby Australian employers were encouraged to select migrants and received payment for each approved person who landed. Understandably, the settlers found it difficult to select, at such a distance from Britain, people they had never met. They were forced to hand over the selection process, and the bounties, to shipping agents, who, working together with shipowners, often crowded the ships as full as possible. The more immigrants they could cram in, the more bounties they received, and so why should they worry too much about the suitability of the immigrants or their comfort during the voyage? An Immigration Board could refuse to authorize payment if an immigrant seemed particularly unsuitable, but, in an age when there was much less official documentation about people than there is now, it was difficult to find out exactly what an individual's circumstances were or to ensure that "certificates of character" were not being forged. But, gradually, in the second half of the nineteenth century, Governments both in Britain and Australia strengthened their control over immigration.

Getting immigrants as far as Australian wharves was one problem; another was matching them to jobs. Settlers from outlying areas were dissatisfied when they had made long, expensive journeys to meet the ships, only to find that the best workers had already been hired. Many new arrivals stayed in the developing townships, not wanting to venture into the bush. Although, even today, Australia is sometimes thought of as having a mainly rural population, in reality the majority of people have always lived in towns and cities, even if few nineteenth-century settlements deserved to be called "cities".

Some Early Australian Cities

This harbour-side scene with ships and a windmill in the background shows some of the inhabitants of early colonial Sydney: soldiers, a "bullocky" driving his team of bullocks, Aborigines, and free settlers. Convicts erected the warehouses and other buildings. Sydney was the largest settlement. Others developed around the Australian coast, including Hobart (1804), Melbourne (1835), Perth (1829) and Adelaide (1836) – all of which later became the capital cities of separate colonies – and Darwin (1869), which developed into the main city of the Northern Territory. In the early twentieth century Canberra was built as the main, or Federal, Capital of Australia.

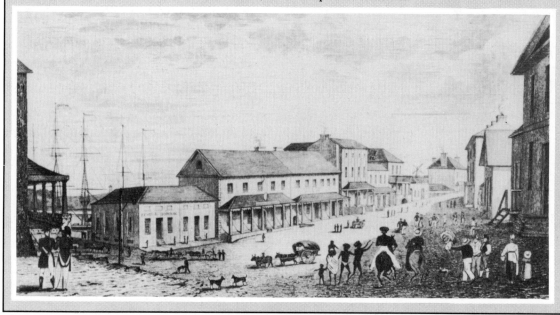

Caroline Chisholm, who worked hard to relieve the "forlorn state of Australian bachelors" by promoting female and family immigration, and improving conditions both on emigrant ships and in the colonies. She was probably the most active woman in colonial public life in the nineteenth century.

Caroline Chisholm, "The Emigrants' Friend"

In early Australian society men far outnumbered women. Unmarried men living in the bush often led unsettled lives, and so female immigration was encouraged. As early as 1832, 50 girls from the Foundling Hospital at Cork were given free passages. But, on arrival, immigrant girls with little money and no contacts were reduced to sleeping in cheap, public lodging houses and parks, often falling in with bad company.

Such girls attracted the attention of Mrs Caroline Chisholm, herself an immigrant, born in Northamptonshire in 1801, who first came to Australia in 1838 when her husband was granted sick leave from the East India Company. In 1841, she met every immigrant ship as it anchored in Sydney Harbour and set up a Female Immigrants' Home in the former convict Hyde Park Barracks. She took large groups of women to country areas where there was a labour shortage, accompanying them in a bullock dray or on her white horse, Captain. Within six years she had helped about 11,000 people.

Caroline Chisholm worked hard in both Australia and Britain to reunite families, including children who had been left in Britain when their parents were transported. In 1850 she helped launch the Family Colonization Loan Society, which helped families migrate and fitted out ships with better accommodation and sanitary facilities. The Society also instructed women about life on board ship:

> **The Passengers are to leave the Poop Deck at Half-past eight in the evening . . . . Water, daily, at half-past six in the morning . . . . The Emigrants are to prepare their food for cooking, and to take it to and receive it from the Cook appointed in the Emigrants' service. This duty should always be done by a man from each mess, as it is not proper for respectable females to go forward among the ship's crew.**
> (Quoted in Margaret Kiddle, *Caroline Chisholm*, Melbourne University Press, 1969, pp. 199-200)

Schemes such as the Family Colonization Loan Society attracted critics as well as supporters. Some people would not repay the loans they had been given once they were safely in Australia. Older settlers, struggling to establish themselves in the bush, complained that newcomers, given too much help, would quickly become rival landowners or that poor Irish immigrants would lower the standard of living, especially as the Irish at this time made up about one quarter of all arrivals. In spite of her critics, Caroline Chisholm persisted with her main aim of establishing "the family" as one of the mainstays of colonial life.

Emigrants' Letters

James Shaw Harding, his wife Eliza and their two children William Thomas, aged eight, and one-year-old Sarah, migrated to South Australia in 1853 on the ship *Mary Green*. In the letters below the original spelling has been kept.

This is James Harding's first letter home in answer to letters he has received from England.

Port Elliot, South Australia, April 23, 1853

My Dear & Beloved Parents and Family,
I have much pleasure in writing to you in answer to your kind and affectionate letters. I am told that the vessel these letters came by had to put into Lisbon with a leak. The 2 newspapers that I received in March were the papers you sent at Christmas. They was only 10 weeks in coming. My income is pretty good. We have sold a great many thousand feet of timber to the government. They fetch it from us as fast as we can cut it. It is a great comfort to me when I think of the learning you gave me. Their is a great many people here that cannot read nor write. I can measure the timber myself. I have a little practice in drawing the plans of houses. I can assure you that I lose no time. Time is money here. Any man that tryes for a living here is sure of it and a good one. Tell Duxford people to come out and not stop there and be starved. We have sent a few parriots feathers. Willy says he wishes he could send his Aunt Sarah a Parriot. Eliza and the dear children join with me in sending their kind love to all of you.

I remain James S. Harding

"News from Australia", by George Baxter, 1854.

And the reply . . .

Duxford, Cambridgeshire, November 5, 1853

My Dear & Beloved Son & Daughter and Grandchildren,
It was with overwhelming joy that we receive your kind and long lookt for letter, and the engraven of the ship with it. We shall have the engraven of the ship put in a frame in remembrance of you. Could you

"News from Home", by George Baxter, 1854.

have seen the tears of joy rowl down our cheeks on receiving your letters, you would never forget it. I had a good crop of barley. The wheat does not yeald very well. Your Sister Charlotte is gone prentice at Luton to be a straw bonnet maker. I hope my dear Boy you will be enabled to look to the Lord in all your undertakings. Your dear Mother and myself are quit please with the hair you have sent. We shall keep it in remberance of the dear children.

We remain your beloved Parents Thomas and Mary Harding
(E.S. Harding, ed., *Letters from the Harding Family of Duxford*, private compilation, Cambridgeshire Collection, Cambridge City Library)

One reason commonly given for migrating to Australia was to be reunited with relatives, a process historians call "chain-migration". Cheerful letters from those who had migrated were a great encouragement to others to try their luck and emigration agents travelled around Britain looking for recruits. Some people, though, felt that they had been misled by glowing reports, as shown by this letter, which appeared in the *Cambridge Chronicle* on 6 March 1875.

Wretched Conditions
of Union Emigrants

Newmarket
One of the unfortunate victims who was persuaded by the emigration agents to break up his home and sail for Queensland last year writes: "When we reached Brisbane I expected to find a comfortable home in the depot by what the papers stated, but I was disappointed. We were huddled together like so many pigs. The way they treat emigrants is a disgrace to any civilised country . . . . Work is not plentiful by a long way . . . . We have taken no harm since we have been in the Colony as far as Victuals [food] is concerned, but the flies and mosquitoes are awful. The worst job I had was to get a house. You make a great deal of talk about your Exning hovels. I am paying nine shillings a week for a worse house than yours, and have to buy our own water. It is a wood house; stands on posts. We have to get up ladders to get in. When you

Settler's bark hut, Gippsland, Victoria, 1886. Clay pipe in his mouth, cat on his lap, and seated on a bush-made stool, this man seems to have most of his worldly goods on display, many of which he would have used to clear his land. On the left, he has a wheelbarrow, a water butt with a splendid bowl of produce on top, and a board against which he would scrub his clothes clean. In front, there is a hatchet and other tools. On the right, there are pannikins, a bucket, a bell on a collar, two saws, and a saddle. Inside his hut, he appears to be using a tree stump as a table. Protruding pieces of wood serve as pegs.

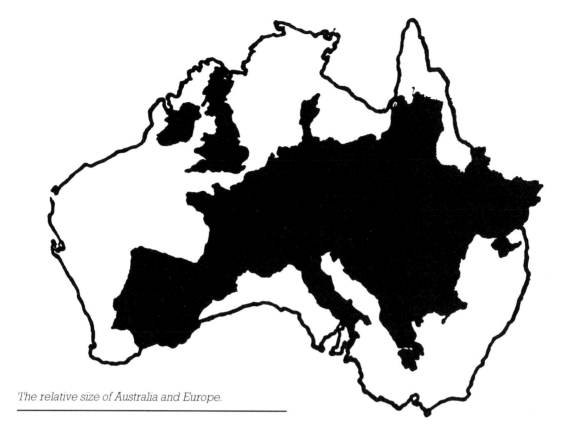

The relative size of Australia and Europe.

hear people lecture about Queensland tell them to speak the truth and not lies, deceiving people."

The British who settled down most easily and comfortably in Australia were usually those who already had contacts, some money, or skills. The Russell family from Kirkcaldy, Scotland, were among many who had the opportunity to put skills to good use. They were experienced engineers and copper-smiths, and by 1846 had established Sydney's first engineering works. Unskilled workers, driven to emigrate by destitution, may well have improved their lives, but they were generally paid less, or worked under more unpleasant conditions, than skilled workers. Also, employers sometimes preferred to hire people from the part of Britain from which they themselves came, for regional loyalties remained strong. The economy went through many booms and depressions, and fortunes could be lost as well as made. Australia may have been a land of opportunity, but it was not a land of complete social and economic equality.

On the map, the Australian continent looks so

large that it is difficult to imagine that the settlement and ownership of land could ever have been a problem. But competition for the most fertile areas, and for those closest to the towns, was very keen. By the mid-1830s overseas demand for fine wool created a boom in the pastoral industry and a demand for more land. In 1829, Governor Darling, hoping to keep the convicts within bounds and also thinking of the close-knit English settlements, tried to confine settlement to 19 areas or "counties". But it was impossible to stop pastoralists from driving their sheep and cattle further and further inland. These people were called "squatters", because they "sat", or "squatted", on their land, known as "runs". Those who took an official view of the situation considered that the squatters were there illegally, even though many squatters were otherwise very respectable people. It took many years of debate and agitation until, in 1847, the squatters were allowed to lease their land for periods of from eight to fourteen years and to buy small but vital sections, such as those parts with a river frontage or the best waterholes. Not all those who wanted land were satisfied, and there

were fears that the squatters were becoming too powerful. The cry went up, "Unlock the lands", which meant "let small farmers have a share of the squatters' runs".

In the 1860s and after, laws were passed allowing applicants who were prepared to live on the land and improve it by clearing the scrub and putting up fences to select and buy pieces of land, whether or not these were already part of squatters' runs. Many squatters felt threatened and were determined to make life difficult for these new "selectors". The squatters employed "dummies", who took up land on their behalf. The dummies could be friends, relations, or even passing strangers. Sometimes the squatters did not even bother to find real people, and simply submitted the selection forms under fictitious names. Dummies often helped the squatter hold on to his land by a practice known as "peacocking". The dummies would select the very best pieces of land on the run – waterholes or river frontages – valuable land that could be compared with the brightest spots on a peacock's feather. No one else would then be able to use the run, and the squatter would become undisputed master.

Many disputes took place between squatters and selectors, but in most areas the squatters won the day because the Australian landscape and climate generally favoured large pastoral runs for animals rather than small farms for crops. There were, of course, exceptions, as in South Australia where the area around Adelaide proved excellent for growing wheat. Nevertheless, Australia continued to "ride on the sheep's back" into the twentieth century.

Women worked hard as pioneers, and not just in the home or as short-term supervisors when their husbands were away with the stock or at the goldfields. London-born Evelyn Maunsell, pioneering in Queensland at the beginning of the twentieth century, remembered:

Loading the Wool. The barque Arabella *was especially designed to come right up on the sands at Cossack, Western Australia. The bullock teams then had four hours until the tide came in to load the baled wool bound for England. On the outward journey from England, the* Arabella *carried railway equipment for unloading at Fremantle, near Perth.*

Sixty or more cows had to be milked twice a day to bring in a living, and, with the men working so hard clearing the land, the women, in addition to doing their housework and looking after new babies, were always in the cow-yards for the milking . . . as far as sheer back-breaking work was concerned, it would be hard to find anyone who contributed more to the opening of the country than those women of the Atherton Tableland.
(Hector Holthouse, *S'pose I Die: the Story of Evelyn Maunsell*, Angus and Robertson, 1973, p. 162)

Professional women also worked long hours. Dr Lilian Violet Cooper, who left her medical practice in Essex, England, in 1891, was Queensland's first registered woman doctor, travelling alone, at night, over rough mountain roads to help her patients. Physical endurance was only part of her story. She also had to work hard to overcome the prejudice against women doctors, which was as marked in Australia as it was in Britain.

It would be wrong to give the impression that the British were the only pioneers. Even in the first days of settlement there were small groups of people from other countries, such as the Greeks brought out to New South Wales at the beginning of the nineteenth century by the Macarthur family to help with their vineyards. Later, in the 1890s, it was the Greek method of cultivating vines that gave the dried fruit industry such a boost, especially in the Renmark-Mildura area of Victoria and South Australia. From the 1830s, German families lived in neat, heavily thatched cottages in the Barossa Valley of South Australia. In the twentieth century their vineyards were to become world famous. The Italian community in the Riverina area of New South Wales can take most of the credit for establishing the fruit-growing industry there.

Peoples other than the British often bore the brunt of opening up difficult areas. The Chinese established market gardens in land dismissed as barren. Kanakas from the Pacific islands toiled in the Queensland sugar-cane plantations, in a tropical heat that many of British origin believed would be too dangerous for anyone used to a milder climate.

5 Those Who Were Impatient to Move: The Goldseekers

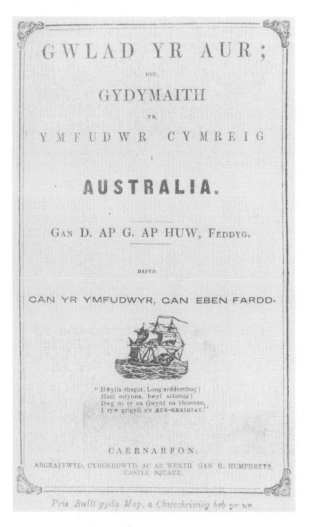

GWLAD YR AUR;

NEU,

GYDYMAITH

YR

YMFUDWR CYMREIG

I

AUSTRALIA.

GAN D. AP G. AP HUW, FEDDYG.

HEFYD

CAN YR YMFUDWYR, GAN EBEN FARDD.

" Hwylia rhagot, Long ardderchog !
Hael estynna, hwyl sidanog !
Dag ni er na Gwynt na thonnau,
I ryw grigyll o'r AUR-GREIGIAU.''

CAERNARFON:

ARGRAFFWYD, CYHOEDDWYD, AC AR WERTH GAN H. HUMPHREYS,
CASTLE SQUARE.

Pris Swllt gyda Map, a Chwecheiniog heb yr un.

THE LAND OF GOLD
or
The companion of the Welsh emigrant
AUSTRALIA
by Dr. Ap G. Ap Huw
also
THE SONG OF THE EMIGRANTS, BY THE POET EBEN
"Sail on, excellent ship!
Generously reach out, satin sail!
Take us in spite of wind and waves
To some part of the GOLDEN ROCKS".

GOLD! The very word had such a ring of excitement about it that thousands left for the gold-fields with scarcely a backward look at their homes. Small quantities of gold had come to light before the 1850s, but they were insignificant in comparison with the huge nuggets found first in New South Wales and then in Victoria. The gold-rushes, which began in 1851, were spectacular examples of "peoples on the move".

Many people died on the ships that headed for

The port of Liverpool dominated the emigrant trade. The White Star Line used North American-built clippers, such as the Red Jacket, *on the Australian route.*

Owing to the low state of the tides the "RED JACKET" will not be able to proceed into the River before the 20th December, on which day she will embark her Passengers.

Liverpool "White Star" Line of Australian Packets.
FOR MELBOURNE.

FORWARDING Passengers to SYDNEY, ADELAIDE, GEELONG, and LAUNCESTON, the celebrated Clipper Ship

"RED JACKET"

M. M. MILWARD, Commander; 2460 tons register, 4000 tons burthen, which has now proved herself to be the fastest Ship in the World, having made during the nine months which have elapsed since she was launched, the following

EXTRAORDINARY PASSAGES :
New York for Liverpool .... 13 days 4 hours.
Liverpool to Melbourne .... 69½ days.
Melbourne to Liverpool .... 73¼ days.
Liverpool to Melbourne and back, 5 months 10 days.
Having circumnavigated the globe in 62 days and 22 hours.

The accommodations afforded to passengers on board the "Red Jacket" are of the most superior description, comprising a very magnificent Poop, Cabin, and Saloon, with a spacious House on deck, eminently adapted for parties and families. The First Class and intermediate State Rooms, and Berths between Decks, are spacious, well ventilated, and liberally provided with every thing which experience can devise for the comfort of passengers. Although so fast a sailer, the "Red Jacket" has proved herself, by the general admission of her passengers, one of the most easy and pleasant ships ever sent to sea, going steadily through the water in all weathers, without that violent motion to which some vessels are liable when under a large spread of canvass.

In consequence of the numerous applications for berths in this ship, the allotment of them will be made in rotation as secured.—Apply to   PILKINGTON & WILSON.

The Red Jacket *meeting ice off Cape Horn on the Great Circle route. Clippers were famous for their sleek lines, tall masts that tilted backwards, and wide spreads of sail. The word "clipper" came from an American expression, "to move at a fast clip". Competition to be one of the fastest ships was intense, and the* Red Jacket *did not touch land from England to Australia.*

Australia during the gold-rushes of the 1850s. Ship owners and agents, greedy for profits or hard pressed by the demand for vessels, squeezed in the passengers. If the ships had called into port more frequently the passengers' diets would have been improved. But the travellers, anxious to reach the gold-fields as soon as possible, and knowing that the voyage could

"Off for the Diggings" at Bathurst, New South Wales, 1851. The cradle for washing the gold free from the dirt is roped on next to the picks, buckets, spade, and bedding.

take anything from two to six months, thought that speed was more important than safety.

Port Phillip Bay became a "complete forest of masts" as immigrants poured in at the rate of 250 a day. Between 1851 and 1861, Victoria's population multiplied seven times, and that of Australia as a whole almost three times, to 1,168,000. Diggers set off for the gold-fields on horseback, or with drays, or on foot, pushing wheelbarrows or carrying heavy swags, breaking their journeys at inns which sprang up along the rough roads, or at "Chisholm's Shakedowns", where families could rest and cook their meals. Even those who were well settled after their migration to the colonies years before were ready to leave secure jobs for the chance to strike it rich. Teachers left their classes to join shopkeepers, postmen, clerks, constables,

shepherds, and thousands of others in the rush to the gold-fields.

The gold-rushes had a dramatic effect on the landscape, much to the astonishment of some Aborigines, who, although they obligingly brought gold nuggets to their bosses' attention, dug over the places again, convinced that White people must really be looking for food. Rows of canvas tents sprang up on the ground where sheep had been grazing only a few weeks before. Traditional Aboriginal grounds were dug up and water supplies diverted and muddied.

Although men outnumbered women on the gold-fields, some families worked their claims together. Living conditions were usually bare and uncomfortable, though stores quickly sprang up to supply all the wants of lucky miners. A young English woman, Ellen Clacy, who followed

"The New Chums' Arrival on a Gold Diggings". The new chums (new arrivals from Britain) are being met by a lively group of diggers (miners), several of whom have been good customers at the illegal "sly grog" shops, judging from the bottles they are waving. Many contemporaries believed that life on the gold fields had an equalizing influence, helping to break down the old English class distinctions, for success now depended more on hard work and luck, rather than on family background or education.

"Australian Gold Diggings", by Edwin Stocquelen, about 1856.

Australian Gold Diggings

Tin-dish washing is generally done beside a stream. The tin dish is round. Into it I placed the "dirt" – digger's technical term for earth or soil – filled the dish up with water, and then with a thick stick commenced making it into a batter. I then let this batter settle, and carefully poured off the water at the top . . . and after doing this several times, the "dirt" of course gradually diminishing, I was overjoyed to see a few bright specks. Puddling is on the same principle as tin-dish washing, only on a much larger scale. Great wooden tubs are filled with the dirt and fresh water, and the former is chopped about in all directions with a spade, so as to set the metal free from the adhesive soil . . . . After having been well beaten in the tubs, the "dirt" is put into the hopper of the cradle, which is then rocked gently. The cradler [holds] a thick stick, ready to break up any clods that may be in the hopper, but which a good puddler would not have sent there. Some of the surface-washing is good, [sometimes] a shaft has to be sunk.

(P. Thompson, ed. *A Lady's Visit to the Gold Diggings of Australia in 1852-53*, written on the spot by Mrs Charles Clacy, Angus and Robertson, London, 1963, extracts from pp. 64, 68, 114)

her emigrant brother out to Australia, visited the gold-fields shortly after her arrival:

The names given to these gullies have a sort of digger's tradition respecting their first discovery. Eagle Hawk derives its name from the number of eagle-hawks seen in the gully before the sounds of pick and shovel drove them away. Murderer's Flat and Choke'em Gully tell their own tale. The Irish clan together in Tipperary Gully. White Horse Gully obtained its name from a white horse whose hoofs flung up the surface ground and disclosed the treasures beneath. In this gully was found the famous "John Bull Nugget" lately exhibited in London. It was sold for £5,000; a good morning's work that! . . .

(Ellen Clacy, *A Lady's Visit to the Gold Diggings of Australia in 1852-53*, pp. 51-2)

There was great rivalry among the diggers to mine faster and, if lucky, to spend more lavishly on horses, carriages and fine clothes than anyone else. Flags flew and bands played as diggers celebrated their finds in extravagant drinking sessions. In 1856, a Mr Cameron rode into Beechworth, Victoria, on a horse called Castor, shod with shoes of gold. This showing-off was the happier side of competition. Less happy was the relationship with Chinese miners.

Landowners had brought Chinese to Australia in the late 1840s, mainly as cheap labour after the

---

A Digger's Letter

To George Muny

Richmond, March 17th, 1852

Dear Friend, We are living in a constant state of excitement – occasioned by the rich discoveries of gold over so large an extent of the country; our population is increasing by thousands weekly . . . . We have Chinese and some of all races, from the East Indies, as well as Yankees and Californians . . . . But gold digging is very hard work, and the heat being very great and the living not first rate (mutton, damper and tea), is very exhausting . . . . The traffic on the road to the "Diggins" is like the traffic on one of the roads leading into London . . .
Yours truly and sincerely,
George Pitty
Stoney Creek, near William's Town

(Quoted in *Cambridge Independent Press*, 14 August, 1852)

---

end of convict transportation. On the gold-fields, local Chinese were joined by thousands more from southern China. The Chinese were often regarded as a group apart. They were criticized for sending their gold back to China instead of investing it in Australia and for staying in their own, mostly male, communities, following customs that seemed strange to Europeans. The Chinese argued that even if these charges were true they were doing no harm because they were only working claims that had already been abandoned by White miners, and they did not force others to share their customs. The White miners paid little attention to these arguments, and sometimes attacked the Chinese, stealing their gold and burning their tents. Some groups of Chinese also suffered at the hands of Aborigines. Those at the Gilbert River during the Queensland diggings of the 1870s, for example, were attacked because they were poorly armed and, travelling on foot rather than on horseback, were less dangerous targets than the more numerous European intruders.

The Chinese presence continued to be a matter of great dispute. It was one of many situations, throughout history, where relatively new arrivals resent competition, real or imagined, from still newer arrivals, especially if they look, dress, and speak differently. The Government restricted coloured immigration, establishing the basis for what later was popularly called the "White Australia policy".

"The Last of England"
"The Last of England" was painted by Ford Madox Brown between 1852 and 1855, when gold-rush emigration from Britain was reaching its peak. But the painting deals with the theme of "exile" rather than that of "hope". Ford Madox Brown wrote:

I have, in order to present the parting scene in its fullest tragic development, singled out a couple from the middle classes, high enough through education and refinement to appreciate all that they are now giving up . . . . The husband broods bitterly over blighted hopes and severance from all that he has been striving for . . .

Ford Madox Brown's sculptor friend, Thomas Woolner, sailed for Australia in July 1852, and this inspired the painting. For a time Ford Madox Brown also thought of emigrating. But Woolner's example was not encouraging, for he had little luck on the gold-fields. Disappointed miners were usually able to find other jobs fairly easily, because the gold-rushes had caused labour shortages

A brooch sent back to England from the gold rushes. "MIZPAH" means "May God protect and keep you while we are apart".

elsewhere, but Woolner decided it would be better to return to England. He sailed home in 1854. It was not "The Last of England" after all!

In the 1850s Victoria produced one-third of the world's gold and, until 1870, gold replaced wool as Australia's principal export. Australian gold also contributed to increased prosperity in Britain. Not everyone was pleased. The social critics Karl Marx and Friedrich Engels, believing that the time would soon be ripe in Britain for the lower classes to seize power from the middle and upper classes, considered that the gold-rushes and emigration had helped delay the expected commercial crisis and the revolution.

The gold-rushes are associated with the 1850s, and particularly with New South Wales and Victoria, but they did not end there. Significant gold discoveries have been made ever since – in New South Wales and Queensland in the late 1850s and 1860s, in the Northern Territory in the 1870s and in Western Australia in the 1890s, and new mines are still being opened today. Mineral discoveries have kept thousands of people on the move, not only from Britain and other countries to Australia, but also within Australia.

6 Contact, Clashes and Co-operation: Aborigines and Newcomers

In 1788 there were probably 300,000 native people scattered throughout Australia. The First Fleet carried just over 1000 British. There seemed to be a reasonable chance of harmony between the First Australians and the newcomers. Governor Phillip ordered that the Aborigines be treated with respect; the Aborigines, though sometimes hostile, were more often curious and cautious, and sometimes proudly confident. Yet, within 150 years of White settlement, the Aboriginal population had declined to about 50,000, a sixth of what it had been in 1788. What impact did the groups have on one another? Why did the Aboriginal population decline?

The Aborigines' response to the coming of White people was very complex. They thought hard about the true nature of the new arrivals, where they had come from, and the purpose of their journey. The British explorer and

---

Early Impressions

In 1862 the explorer John McDouall Stuart and his party met a group of Aborigines in the Roper River region of the Northern Territory. Each group found the other both potentially threatening and rather comic. Each felt that it had done its best to be friendly, even if the encounter as a whole was rather disappointing.

Buludja, an Aboriginal woman, tells the Aborigines' side of the story:

> The first time that Old Cordil ever saw a horse . . . he was terrified and ran away . . . but the tribe had learnt a little wisdom and, in order to make peace, they took a coolamon of fish up to the white camp. This pleased the white men very much and they gave them some small pieces of cloth. The blacks knew this was some kind of present but did not know what to do with it. To show them, one of the men put a piece of white cloth to his nose and blew into it. The blacks thought this was great fun. They followed the white men up the creek to the head of the water-course, and again frightened the horses. But this time they got nothing at all and they went sadly away, continuing to burn the country as they went to kill the

devil-devil left behind by the white man's presence.

(Quoted in H.E. Thoneman, *Tell the White Man. The Life Story of an Aboriginal Lubra*, 1949, pp. 24-5)

The White explorers' side of the story:

> **Tuesday July 1 1862, River Chambers**
> Before sunrise the natives again made their appearance, sixteen in number, with small spears . . . . Thring opened the lips of one of the horses and showed them his teeth . . . they ran off the moment they saw them.
>
> **Wednesday August 13, Roper River**
> As we were saddling, one native and two women made their appearance and came close to the camp . . . . The man made signs he would like to get a fish-hook by bending his forefinger and placing it in his mouth imitating the method of catching fish. I gave him one with which he was much pleased; I also gave a cotton handkerchief to each of the women, one of whom no sooner got it than she held out the other hand, calling out "more, more, more" – with that request I did not feel inclined to comply.

(John McDouall Stuart, *Explorations Across the Continent of Australia, 1861-2*, Melbourne, 1863, pp. 41; 64-5)

administrator George Grey showed some understanding of the conclusion many Aborigines reached:

> Never having the idea of quitting their own land, [the Aborigines] cannot imagine others doing it – and thus, when they see white people suddenly appear in their country, and settling themselves down in particular spots, they imagine that they must have formed an attachment for this land in some other state of existence, and hence conclude the settlers were at one period black men, and their own relations.
>
> (George Grey, *Journals of Two Expeditions of Discovery*, Vol. 2, London, 1941, p. 302)

This helps to explain why some Aboriginal groups were so puzzled and disappointed when the newcomers did not react as relations should. Whether or not White people were really returned relations (and not all Aborigines thought they were), they were concerned that the newcomers lacked some of the basic social values. Sharing food and goods was central to Aboriginal society, but White people wanted to keep things to themselves. Sometimes the Aborigines speared the White settlers' cattle, not to eat, but to try to force White people to share.

The White settlers rarely took the Aborigines' intimate links with the land into account when they established their "runs" or "stations" on tribal grounds. They became very alarmed when the Aborigines speared their sheep and cattle, or frightened them so often that the animals lost condition. In England such "poaching" or deliberate damage to another's property could be punished by transportation or even death. The

Driving away evil spirits that might have followed a visitor. Part of the "Nugwearipa" ritual, Arnhem land, photographed in the 1950s. A few tribes did not make contact with White people until the twentieth century.

newcomers lost no time in retaliating, sometimes poisoning the Aborigines' food and water, or shooting them down as if they were game. This was warfare as the Aborigines understood it, and they, in turn, speared shepherds and set fire to huts and grass.

The officials who looked into these disputes seldom heard the Aborigines' side of the story, although there were exceptions. In June 1838 the overseer of a property near Myall Creek, north of Sydney, noticed that birds of prey were hovering over a clump of bushes. When he went to investigate he found the mangled, shot, decapitated, and half-burnt remains of 28 Aborigines, some of whom were children. The slaughter may have been in retaliation for the deaths of white hutkeepers and shepherds but, even so, the murder was particularly callous. Eleven white men were brought to court, tried, and acquitted. In their defence they told Sydney's Principal Gaoler:

> **They were not aware that in destroying the aboriginals they were violating the law . . . as it (according to their belief) had been done so frequently in the colony before.**
> ("Despatches Relative to the Massacre of Aborigines", Parliamentary Papers, Vol. XXXIV, 1839)

"Police and Aborigines Clash.", by G.C. Mundy, 1853.

Governor Thomas Davey's proclamation in Van Diemen's Land, 1816, telling the Aborigines about the British system of justice.

But Governor Gipps was not satisfied and ordered a retrial. This time the men were found guilty and seven were hanged.

Van Diemen's Land saw years of conflict between the Aborigines and White people. In the early years of settlement, supplies were so short that convicts were allowed to look for food in the bush, with instructions not to harm the Aborigines. But many convicts, through ignorance, viciousness, or because they had been ill-treated by their guards, thought that, in turn, it was acceptable to abuse and kill native men, women and children. This was a taste of things to come.

By the time Governor George Arthur arrived in Van Diemen's Land in 1824, free people had begun to migrate there. But in the 1820s, it was not safe to settle in much of the colony. Escaped convicts-turned-bushrangers roamed the hills, and Aborigines burnt settlers' huts, spearing the inmates. The settlers had come in search of good pasture for sheep, but the land they chose was often the very land already occupied and valued by the Aborigines. The Aborigines' defence of their land sometimes forced the White settlers to move, or made them very anxious, though the Aborigines also suffered in the process. Food ran

short in ways that White people did not understand. To European eyes, there seemed to be plenty of animals to go round, but some Aboriginal groups customarily ate female animals while others preferred male animals. Intensive hunting made the supplies of the right kinds of food less predictable. Aborigines also suffered when White pressure drove members of one tribe into the territory of another. White settlers introduced tuberculosis and other diseases to which the Aborigines, so long isolated from the rest of the world, had little resistance. In addition to deaths in conflict and from disease, the Aboriginal population declined because fewer children were born or survived when tribes were broken up or on the run.

Relations between European men and Aboriginal women also caused tension and dislocation. Aboriginal women were sometimes offered by their tribes to White men as a friendly gesture, only to find that instead of being treated kindly as relations, they were cheated and abused. Some Europeans simply abducted Aboriginal women and children, keeping or abandoning them at will. Formal marriages between Europeans and Aborigines or part-Aborigines were permissible in the eyes of the law and Christianity, but they remained the exception rather than the rule. When Fanny Cochrane (1835-1903), the daughter of a Tasmanian sealer and an Aboriginal woman, married a European called Smith, the couple and their child apparently lived happily on a

Tasmanian part-Aboriginal Fanny Cochrane Smith records Aboriginal songs in 1903. She was known to Truganini and, like her, survived the destruction of Aboriginal communities in the nineteenth century.

Truganini

Truganini occupies a special place in the history of Tasmanian Aborigines. Born in 1812, she was abducted by Whites when she was young and spent most of her life with them, even though her mother, sister, and the man who was to be her husband all died or were killed as a result of White contact. In 1835 she helped George Robinson round up her people, thinking at first that this was the best plan for them, and for a while she lived on Flinders Island. Later she criticized Robinson. After leaving Flinders Island she joined other Aborigines in raids on settlers' huts, although she continued to have European friends.

Truganini died in Hobart in 1876. At the time, she was called "the last of the Tasmanian Aborigines" because she was the last of her generation to die in the land where she had been born. Other Tasmanian Aborigines were still living, but no longer in Tasmania. For many years Truganini's skeleton, or at least the skull, which was almost certainly hers, was on display in a museum in Tasmania. Some people wanted it kept there, though not necessarily on display, because of its rare scientific interest, and also as a grim reminder of the Aborigines' sufferings. Others, especially those in the Aboriginal community, asked that the skeleton be given a dignified burial or cremation following Aboriginal traditions. After years of debate the skeleton was cremated in 1976 and the ashes cast over the sea, not far from Truganini's birthplace. Today, descendants of Aboriginal Tasmanians still live in Tasmania and on islands in Bass Strait.

"The Conciliation", by Benjamin Dutterau, 1840. George Robinson is seen here in the 1830s with some of the Aborigines he tried to save, not realizing the stress he was placing on them by trying to replace their customs and values with European culture. Truganini (also spelt Trucanini), the girl on the right with an arm and leg raised, was the longest lived of all this group.

Truganini, now in European-style clothing, with one of her British friends: poet and lawyer, John Woodcock Graves (1795-1886), the author of the song "John Peel".

Some British officials disapproved of the exercise and were not nearly as eager as Governor Arthur, who left his wife in childbirth to superintend the plan. One police magistrate, Edward Dumaresq, deliberately led his party down the roads instead of into the bush. In any case, the local Aborigines, being so familiar with the land, slipped through the net.

Persuasion was tried next, and by 1835 the missionary George Robinson had won the Aborigines' confidence sufficiently to encourage 200, all who remained of an estimated population of 4000-7000, to move to Flinders Island in the notoriously rough Bass Strait. This enforced migration proved too much for the natives. Christianity and British schooling were no substitute for their former traditions. Severed from their tribal units and customs, most of them died. The full-blooded Aboriginal population of Van Diemen's Land was virtually wiped out by White settlement. The same was true, sooner or later, of the full-blooded Aborigines in the Monaro and Molonglo districts of New South Wales, in parts of north Queensland, in the area around Swan River in Western Australia, and in many other places. The exact number of Aborigines is difficult to estimate, for they were not included in the census of Australian people until 1971 and no careful surveys were made of those with mixed Aboriginal-European ancestry. But there is no doubt that in many areas the traditional foundations of Aboriginal society had been destroyed.

Just as the White settlers had to decide in particular circumstances whether they should ignore the Aborigines, accept them, or fight them off, so the Aborigines had to choose in certain instances whether to go into White society, stay as far away as possible, or incorporate only items such as iron tools, which would be useful to them in their traditional ways of life. Different groups had different reactions. Both the first Australians and the newcomers faced a frontier, where much was unknown. Some Aborigines were drawn to major towns, eager to experience new foods, clothes, weapons and to make friends with other Aborigines who gathered in "fringe" camps on the outskirts of the towns. Others were refugees from the insecurity of life in the bush, though life in the towns was by no means free of danger: disease, malnutrition, alcohol, tobacco, poor housing, unemployment and ill-treatment from White people took a heavy toll.

While these terrible hardships should not be

Government grant of land for the rest of their lives. But many other children born to White fathers and Aboriginal mothers were neglected or even killed.

In 1830, Governor George Arthur organized what became known as the "Black Line". The aim was to end all conflict and to save the remaining Aborigines by capturing them and resettling them on nearby islands. A long line of 3000 men, including some Aborigines brought especially from New South Wales to help with the tracking, was stretched across the island, with the intention of driving the Tasmanian natives into the "net".

underestimated, it is also important to remember instances of co-operation and affection between individual Whites and Aborigines. Many escaped convicts, victims of shipwreck, explorers, and children lost in the bush were looked after by Aborigines when they might otherwise have died. The escaped convict William Buckley (1780-1856) lived happily with the Aborigines for 32 years, and had almost forgotten the English language when his former countrymen found him. The explorer Edward John Eyre (1815-1901) would almost certainly not have survived his marathon walk across the Great Australian Bight without the support of his Aboriginal companion, Wylie. "Black-trackers" helped find criminals or people lost in bush country, and many a settler relied heavily on black stockmen who, already knowing a great deal about animal behaviour, became experts with sheep and cattle.

Although many White settlers treated the Aborigines as nothing more than cheap labour, or patronized them, considering them inferior, there were also times when both Aborigines and Whites genuinely appreciated one another's company. Happy relationships were recorded by Mrs Evelyn Maunsell, an immigrant from Ilford near London, who had first-hand experience of pioneering life in Queensland:

> **My son Ron was born on 8th May 1922 . . . .**
> **That night the blacks asked us to come to the**
> **creek to see the big new corroboree [dance]**
> **about the arrival of the first white baby at**
> **Wrotham Park.**
> (Hector Holthouse, *S'pose I Die: The Story of Evelyn Maunsell*, Angus and Robertson, Sydney, 1973, pp. 176 and 212)

By the late nineteenth century the colonial governments were aware of the damage that White occupation had inflicted on the

The first Aboriginal cricket team, December 1866. Some of the men shown here made up the first Australian cricket team to tour England. They played 43 matches, including one at Lords where they led in the first innings and lost the match by only 55 runs.

Aborigines. Believing that the Aboriginal population would continue to decline, they introduced a policy of protection to "smooth the pillow of the dying race". From the 1890s special Aboriginal reserves run by government officials and missions were established which White people, except for those working with the Aborigines, needed special permission to enter. But life on the reserves was very far removed from traditional life. While some Christian missions genuinely protected and helped the Aborigines, others set out to abolish tribal customs. Many Aborigines lived in insanitary conditions, existing on poor quality food rations. In their former life, Aborigines moved camp and left their waste behind where it soon rotted in the earth. Now tin cans and other debris piled up around them.

From the 1950s, the Government began a policy of assimilation, one feature of which was to educate Aboriginal and White children together in the same classrooms. Even so, it was not until 1967 that the Australian constitution was amended to admit Aborigines to full citizenship. Neville Thomas Bonner was elected Senator for Queensland in 1971, the first Aborigine to be elected to any Parliament in Australia. Charles Nelson Perkins, born at Alice Springs in 1936, was, in 1973, the first Aborigine to graduate with a Bachelor of Arts degree. Kathleen Jean Mary Walker, born on Stradbroke Island off the Queensland coast in 1920, reached a wide audience with poems, stories and reminiscences including *My People* and *Stradbroke Dreamtime*. These three were among many who were very concerned about the problems that still faced the Aborigines.

One of the most important problems was that of the ownership and use of land. In the 1960s Aboriginal workers in the Northern Territory walked off cattle stations, many of which were British owned, beginning a long campaign for better conditions and to have their traditional lands returned to them. Although they did not achieve all their aims, their actions led many Aboriginal groups to take more positive, active steps to improve their condition. The question of Aboriginal rights was now firmly before Australia – and, indeed, before the world.

In 1971 a group of Aborigines sent a formal complaint to the United Nations:

From the time of the first settlement to date . . . the Crown has blatantly taken our land without treaty, without purchase and without compensation of any kind . . .

At this time the Aboriginal population was approximately 150,000, about 25,000 of whom were of full Aboriginal descent. Since then, some land has been returned, but not all their demands have been satisfied. The discovery of coal and such minerals as uranium on especially important Aboriginal sites has resulted in a complex clash of interests, which, in many areas, has still to be resolved.

7 Landscape and Life

The early British settlers who thought that they had come upon a landscape virtually untouched by people were mistaken. The Aborigines controlled their environment by "fire-stick" farming. They used fire to drive out the game from the bush, burn off old vegetation, and encourage new growth to attract game once more. This was most effective in regions of good rainfall, where vegetation sprang up quickly, the very regions that the British came to value for pastoral industries.

> bili gurda duri-nirara manalju
>   wudgjulmundu jigulju
> nirana-mardji boiul-woiul mara
> duri-nirara gandji wundjanu nirara-mardji
>   jimagan
> narana magar
> [n is an ng sound]
>
> "They are lighting small fires, men of the
>   barramundi clans ...
> Lighting small fires, burning along through
>   the grass and foliage ...
> Fire burning low down among the grasses,
>   burning the clumps so that new shoots
>   may come ..."
>
> (Ronald M. Berndt, *Love Songs of Arnhem Land*,
> University of Chicago Press, 1978, pp. 102, 223)

Before 1788, no horse, or sheep, or cow, in fact no animal with a hoof (kangaroos have claws), had ever trodden on Australian soil. Imported plants and animals had a dramatic impact on the environment. The new settlers and the well-intentioned Acclimatization Societies, who brought in and encouraged living things from the "Old World", could never have imagined the consequences. Sheep- and cattle-grazing improved the land in some areas but in others the heavy hooves and intensive grazing encouraged weeds instead of grass. Imported rabbits, too,

> ## Unwelcome Imports
>
> An unlucky importation was the Scotch thistle, which a Scotch lady near here [Bathurst, New South Wales] planted in her garden and which took so kindly to the country that it grows everywhere. The paddock is half full of it.
> (D. Adams, ed., *The Letters of Rachel Henning (1853-1882)*, Penguin Books, 1969, p. 70)
>
> One day [in 1908] I went down to inspect the crop and found rabbits there in thousands. Two days later there was no sign of my corn crop and the roots had been eaten out of the ground.
> (Samuel Shumack, *An autobiography or Tales and Legends of Canberra Pioneers*, Australian National University Press, Canberra, 1977, p. 161)

caused devastation. This is one reason why so many graziers were "nomadic": pasture exhaustion or soil erosion forced them to keep looking for more or better land. Many imports that changed the environment arrived accidentally. Weed seeds were embedded in sheep's fleeces or mixed in with grain. But once established, Scotch thistles, prickly pear, dandelions, and blackberries all became plagues.

The story was not a simple one of White people wiping out native flora and fauna. Some imports actually encouraged the native wildlife. The cattle ate out the tall grasses, leaving shorter grasses which were more acceptable not only to the sheep but also to the grey kangaroos and wallabies. Cockatoos and galahs flocked to fruit ripening in orchards and suburban gardens. Also, indigenous animals often multiplied when the Aborigines stopped hunting them.

The White settlers' impact on the land was also linked with technological developments. In the 1870s and 1880s, for example, there was a boom

Dramatic changes in the landscape made within five years. The same view of land owned by the Turner family in Augusta, Western Australia, shown in 1836 and 1840. Note the extent of tree-felling and ring-barking, and the lengths of post-and-rail fencing made from the timber.

in wire fencing. As one modern writer, Noel Butlin, has observed,

> A population of less than one million people, most of them urban dwellers, had, in the course of twenty years, strung ten million miles [16 million kilometres] of wire around the New South Wales countryside.
> (N.G. Butlin, "The Growth of Rural Capital, 1860-90" in A. Barnard, ed., *The Simple Fleece*, Melbourne, 1962, p. 333)

When British settlers came to Australia, they brought their most treasured possessions, such as leather-bound volumes of the Bible and Shakespeare, watches and waistcoats, and even pianos. They also came with many ideas about the ways society should be organized. They had ideas about laws; a belief in the virtue of the Christian faith and of hard work; codes of ways to behave in private and in public; ideas about the

Cornwall in South Australia. The parlour in a miner's home. Cornish immigrants, attracted by rich copper finds in the Yorke Peninsula region, transplanted the architectural style of their Cornish cottages and their tastes in furnishing. During the 1870s, South Australia replaced Cornwall as the busiest copper region in the British Empire.

aims people ought to have in life. Of course, not every British settler held exactly the same views, but most would have accepted the idea that British civilization had much to offer this untamed land.

Middle- and upper-class English manners had a strong influence on etiquette in the equivalent colonial social circles.. In 1833 Edward John Eyre, accustomed to the genteel refinements of life in a Yorkshire rectory, was relieved to find that on an Australian farm more than a day's journey from Sydney,

"Scotland" in Tasmania. Government House, Hobart, recorded in the very early days of photography, 1856, was built in the "baronial" style of Balmoral castle, the Derwent River serving as a Scottish loch.

... the [Dumaresq] family always dined late and always dressed for dinner, keeping up good old English habits in this and many other respects

(Jill Waterhouse, ed., *Edward Eyre's Autobiographical Narrative of Residence and Exploration in Australia*, 1832-1839, Caliban Press, London, 1984, p. 39)

Colonial social life could be very grand indeed. Annabella Boswell described a dinner party held in 1843:

The table was laid very handsomely for eighteen persons . . . . There were two silver wine coolers with light wines and branch candlesticks with wax candles, and four silver side dishes. Bruce and the butler waited, and we had four footmen in livery. I felt quite dazzled, as I had never been at so splendid an entertainment before.

(Morton Herman, ed., *Annabella Boswell's Journal*, Angus and Robertson, Sydney, 1965, p. 63)

British influence on Australian education ran

Australians, though, did not simply follow along behind the British. They developed ideas and traditions of their own, from popular songs to politics. "The Man From Snowy River", a bush ballad written by "Banjo" Paterson in 1890 about the courage and endurance of men and horses, became the first Australian best-seller and was as well known in schools as any British poem. Paterson also adapted "Waltzing Matilda" from a traditional source, using words such as "jumbuck" (sheep) and "billabong" (freshwater lagoon) which were distinctively Australian.

Although Australian parliamentary and legal systems were largely modelled on British systems Australia did not copy "the Mother country" in all respects, and indeed introduced some political reforms ahead of Britain. The right to vote was extended to women over the period 1894-1908, whereas this did not happen in Britain until 1918 and 1928.

very deep. Debates about the place of religion in schools were imported, as were the ways in which the educational institutions were organized. The King's Schools at Parramatta and Sydney, established in 1832, were run by the Anglican church on English public school lines. Non-conformists, such as Presbyterians, and Roman Catholics also established private schools. Stones from English schools such as Eton were proudly placed in the walls of Australian schools. Scottish and English universities influenced the organization of Australia's first universities, founded at Sydney and Melbourne in the middle of the nineteenth century. Government schools for young children were based on the Irish National System, with the same text books. Young Irish-born Samuel Shumack, living at isolated Ginninderra in the 1860s, used the same schoolbooks he would have had in Ireland:

It was the rule after supper to read aloud some tale from the Irish National School books, which were used in all schools at that time, or the *London Spelling Book*.

Sports were also imported, and Australians soon began to challenge the British at their own games – in particular cricket. In 1882 at the Oval, London, the English team was devastated by Australian bowling. The *Sporting Times* lamented the death of English cricket saying that the body had been cremated and the ashes sent to Australia. Both countries still compete for the "Ashes". In the early days of radio, Australian interest in cricket matches being played in England was so intense that at least one announcer in Australia clicked pencils together to try to give "realistic" sound effects of ball on bat as part of his "live" commentary, even though he was entirely dependent on news being relayed by telegraph!

8 Moving through the Twentieth Century

At the beginning of the twentieth century the British Empire extended over a quarter of the world's land surface and a fifth of its population, including Australia. Although on New Year's Day 1901 the Australian colonies had become states in a new federation called the Commonwealth of Australia, loyalty to Britain remained strong. The new Australian flag incorporated the Union Jack as well as the stars of the Southern Cross. Although three-quarters of the population was born in Australia, most of them were children of immigrants from the British Isles.

After Federation, the "White Australia policy" was strengthened, prohibiting settlement by non-Europeans. At the same time, immigration from Britain was encouraged by "assisted passage" schemes. These schemes took advantage of the already well-established links with Britain. They also sprang from fears that unrestricted immigration might result in other, less friendly, powers taking over Australia. In addition, it was believed that an Australian population from roughly the same background would produce a harmonious society, relatively free from the racial tensions that scarred many other countries. In 1912 almost 90,000 immigrants entered Australia, the highest intake since the gold-rushes of the 1850s.

Ticket from a 1914 campaign to attract young immigrants, just before the outbreak of the First World War.

BRITISH LADS FOR AUSTRALIA.

This Ticket admits ONE LAD over 14
TO THE

GREAT MASS MEETING for LADS

AT THE

People's Palace, Mile End Road, Whitechapel, E.,
TUESDAY, JULY 28th, 1914, at 8 p.m.

SUBJECT:

Farm Life in Australia: Its Advantages and Prospects.

ADDRESSES BY
Mr. COLIN BELL,
Mr. JOHNNY SUMMERS,
and Mr. THOS. E. SEDGWICK.

Biograph Films.   Band.   Flashlight Photo.

An Early-Twentieth-Century Immigrant

My childhood was spent in the north of England, the Co. of Durham, right in the centre of the coal-mining industries, growing up in a cloud of black smoke and blacker coal-dust.

Upon attaining the age of fourteen, I automatically became a source of extra income for the upkeep of the family, no more schooling.

Nowhere could any job be found for a boy except at the mines, and so, that is where I went, to do an 11-hour shift for 5 days, Monday to Friday inclusive, and 7 hours on Saturday ...

I remember many strikes, and too many times of not having enough to eat, and it was that, mainly, that was the cause of my father deciding to get out of the Old Dart, and start a new life in one of the colonies. The final decision was Australia.

We landed in Australia sometime in July 1913, and I found myself working in a coal mine once more, but a mine where [a man did not] have to crawl about on his hands and knees, and where he could earn wages that would eventually allow him to own his own home.

And the sun, – we had never seen so much of it, the surfing beaches, the wonders of the bush ...

(J.N.I. Dawes and L.L. Robson, *Citizen to Soldier: Australia before the Great War. Recollections of the Members of the first A.I.F.*, Melbourne University Press, 1977, pp. 80-1)

Raising funds for the war effort, Sydney Cricket Ground, October 1914.

When World War I broke out in 1914 many British immigrants joined the Australian-born soldiers in the Australian Imperial Force. Involvement in the war was not welcomed by everyone, but the majority felt deeply patriotic about Britain and her Empire.

Although both of my parents had been born in S.[outh] A.[ustralia] they still referred to England as the "home country", they were the most patriotic Britishers. To them, the British were superior people, noted particularly for

their integrity and wise rule. During my boyhood [I was born on 2.12. 1897] British military exploits were extolled. I can still remember a steel engraving of Sir Garnett Wolseley [with medals etc.] hanging in our drawing room. To my parents, the British Navy was superb and invincible. I never heard any

reference, either at home or at school, to the evils of Colonialism.

(J.N.I. Dawes and L.L. Robson, *Citizen to Soldier*, pp. 54-5)

Australia's participation in two world wars influenced the way her inhabitants thought about themselves. Particularly arduous battles such as Gallipoli in the First World War and the fighting in New Guinea in the Second World War helped give them a sense of identity. Australians were no longer simply transplanted Britons: they had begun to develop traditions of their own. But this applies mainly to the ways in which Australians of predominantly British origin began to think about themselves in relation to other countries. Other Australians saw the matter rather differently, as Buludja, an Aboriginal woman from the Northern Territory, explained:

Many of the white men left this country to join in the fight. They went to fight the Germans, which I suppose was a different tribe of white

Orphans from Dr Barnardo's Home arriving in 1924 to settle in Australia. Between 1921 and 1950 donations from the public supported about 2000 such children.

men. We had a German working here for a long time, but we did not see any difference between him and the others. I suppose the white men do not see much difference between one of our tribes and another . . . . I cannot understand how your wars last so long unless you run away and hide. When I asked one of your white men about this, he told me that some soldiers dug holes in the ground and lived in them, so you could not shoot them . . . . When we fight we use our weapons and the war is soon over.

(Quoted in H.E. Thonemann, *Tell the White Man*, Sydney, 1949, pp. 73-5)

Buludja's puzzlement was not shared by all Aborigines, some of whom fought overseas or joined patrols in Australia. Her view is, nevertheless, a reminder that it is difficult to generalize about the influence of events even as large as two world wars on Australian society. The discussion about the extent to which Australia was becoming a nation, able to stand on her own feet without too much support from Britain, meant little to Buludja, who felt there was still so much to be done to bridge the gaps in understanding between peoples within the Australian continent.

Wars and the needs of industry stimulated the demand for migrants. "Men, Money and Markets" became an Australian catch-cry in the 1920s. Britain and the Dominions worked together on schemes to settle the Empire's vast spaces, to provide more labour and larger markets for both agricultural and manufactured goods. Australia gained over 260,000 people from Britain in the 1920s, about 80 per cent of whom were nominated as suitable settlers by friends or employers and so qualified for assisted passages. The scheme's success was limited. Only a small proportion settled outside the towns and the worldwide economic depression of the late 1920s and early 1930s undermined the scheme. In 1935 former Prime Minister William Morris Hughes expressed a widely held concern when he declared that it was a case of "populate or perish", meaning that if Australia's population did not

increase her industries would die and, worse, some other power might be tempted to invade her vast open spaces.

After World War II a census showed that there were only 7½ million inhabitants, and that the birth-rate was not high enough to ensure Australia's growth, particularly in secondary industries. Schemes to bring out European war refugees, British ex-servicemen and women and their families, and British migrants who only had to pay a fare of £10 per person, together stimulated one of the largest migrations in the history of the southern hemisphere. The 1947 population of 7½ million had risen to 12½ million by 1969.

On arrival in Australia many twentieth-century migrants were temporarily housed in hostels. They were often disappointed with conditions there and with housing shortages, especially if they had set their hearts on owning their own homes as soon as they arrived.

The British contribution to Australia's population growth was greater in the 40 or so

Post Second World War immigration. A computer-drawn pie-chart, showing the origins of people who came to Australia between July 1947 and June 1970 with the intention of settling.

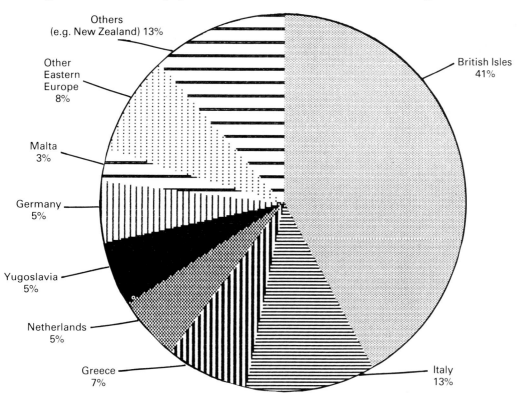

Others (e.g. New Zealand) 13%

Other Eastern Europe 8%

Malta 3%

Germany 5%

Yugoslavia 5%

Netherlands 5%

Greece 7%

British Isles 41%

Italy 13%

years after World War II than it had been in any earlier 40-year period. But, with large numbers of migrants coming from war-torn Europe after 1945, the British no longer formed the majority of newcomers. Immigrants from Italy came in ever increasing numbers, and the city of Melbourne claimed to have the largest Greek population outside Greece – and, indeed, outside Athens. Like the British, these immigrants were conscious of their regional origins – whether they came from the north or south of a particular country, for example – and so they added a host of different traditions to Australian life. Post-war immigration enabled Australia to launch many major projects, such as the Snowy River Hydro-Electric and Irrigation Scheme, which, by means of reservoirs and tunnels, turned a river around, making it flow into dry inland areas instead of into the sea. In the years following the end of the Second World War there were increasing signs that the relationship between Britain and Australia was changing. In foreign policy and defence Australia looked less to Britain, who was gradually withdrawing her forces from East of Suez, and more to the United States. Trading patterns changed, too. Australia's dependence on imported manufactured goods declined as her own industries grew. Australia also began to export more to Japan, a ready market for her minerals, than to Britain. At about the same time Britain turned her attention to her own North Sea oil-fields and to the European Economic Community, which she joined in 1972.

Australians no longer looked at the world through predominantly British eyes. In the 1960s, for example, the New South Wales Government advised teachers to substitute the term "Near North" for what had been known as the "Far East", a change applauded by all Australian schoolchildren, who had previously been tied to British perceptions of the geographical world.

As Australia's links with her northern neighbours increased, the Australian Labor Party set out, in 1973, to change the "White Australia policy" by specifying that discrimination on the grounds of race, skin colour, or nationality was to be avoided. Even so, high unemployment levels and a fear that the world's population was already growing at too fast a rate put the brakes on many immigration schemes. The restrictions placed on the numbers of migrants admitted to Australia also applied to British migrants.

"Advance Australia Fair" replaced "God Save the Queen" in the 1970s as Australia's national anthem, although the latter is still used in the presence of royalty. In 1986, the Australia Act confirmed Australia's status as an independent

Queen Elizabeth the Queen Mother and the Surf Life-Savers of Manly, Sydney, 1958. In 1954 Her Majesty Queen Elizabeth II was the first reigning British monarch to visit Australia. Her son, Charles, later spent six months at Timbertop, the mountain branch of Geelong Grammar School, Victoria. Royal visits were a regular feature of Australian life.

Northern hemisphere traditions find a happy home in Australia, even if the setting – in this case Bondi Beach, Sydney – is very different.

nation by ending the British Parliament's power to make laws for Australia. The British monarch remains monarch of Australia because Australia wants this to be the case, not because Britain declares it should be so. Republicans hope for the day when even this link is cut, arguing that the British monarchy is irrelevant now that Australia is constitutionally independent and has so many non-British inhabitants. Other Australians believe that at least some traditional links with Britain are worth preserving, and that, for the time being at least, the existing situation gives Australia the best of both worlds.

Glossary

Aborigine from the Latin *ab origine* meaning "from the beginning". It can be used to describe the "first inhabitant" of any area in the world, but, with a capital letter "A" is more commonly applied to an original inhabitant of Australia. "Aboriginal" may be used instead of "Aborigine". The word "black" appears in terms such as "black-tracker", an Aborigine who is good at following tracks in the bush. Today, more and more English-speaking descendants of the first inhabitants refer to themselves as "Koori" or by other words of their own, in preference to any term of European origin.

assignment the allocation of convicts to free settlers.

coolamon a wood or bark container, used by the Aborigines for carrying food and water.

dominions self-governing countries of the British Commonwealth.

Dreaming the name in English for the sacred time of the Aborigines' ancestors who made the world. Even though the creation period is past, the Dreaming goes on forever, for the ancestors remain as rocks, trees or other features of the environment, still full of life-giving power.

emancipist an ex-convict; also called an "expiree".

European this word is used to cover the British, except where it is clear that it only includes people from mainland Europe. Also used as another word for "White".

exclusive a person opposed to giving convicts full rights in the community; also called an "exclusionist".

federation a system of government whereby a number of states are linked to form one nation. The central, or federal, government controls such matters as defence, and the states control their own internal matters, such as law and order. Australia became a federation, known as the Commonwealth of Australia, in 1901. After this date, the colonies became states.

indigenous belonging naturally to a country, not imported.

Kanaka a South Sea Islander, especially one working in Queensland on sugar plantations.

larceny a legal word for theft.

native a term used for both Aborigines and White people born in Australia. It is usually possible to tell from the context which group is meant. It also applies to the plants and animals that grow naturally in Australia, as opposed to those imported in the last few hundred years.

pastoralist a sheep or cattle farmer; also called a "grazier".

pauper a very poor person; a person supported by charity.

run land, usually for grazing sheep and cattle. Other Australian terms for this include "property", "selection" and "station".

seditious conspiracy plotting to undermine the authorities or cause a rebellion.

selector a person who chooses a piece of Crown land – that is, land owned by the State, and who, by paying for it in instalments and abiding by certain regulations, comes to own it.

steerage that part of a ship allocated to passengers travelling at the cheapest rate.

squatter a person who occupies land without having a formal or legal right to do so; more generally, a grazier with large flocks of sheep.

swag a bundle of personal belongings, often rolled in a blanket, carried by a bush-traveller called a "swaggie" or "swagman".

ticket-of-leave a licence giving a convict restricted freedom before his or her sentence had been completed.

totem part of the natural world – an animal, plant or other thing – which has special significance for the Aborigines, linking them with their ancestors. It is not a word used by the Aborigines themselves.

transportation the process of being taken to, and living in, a convict settlement as a penalty for crime.

tribe a group of Aborigines who speak the same language and know one another.

Date List

(Entries in parentheses refer to individuals mentioned in this book.)

B.C.

40,000   The Aborigines are settled in Australia. Their culture is already old when the Egyptian king Tutankhamen, is placed in his tomb, or Stonehenge is built in Britian.

A.D.

1577-80   Francis Drake becomes the first Englishman to enter the Pacific.

1688   British sailor William Dampier lands on Australia's west coast. Sailors from many other lands were also familiar with parts of Australia's coastline.

1760   George III becomes King.

1770   Captain James Cook lands on Australia's east coast.

1783   Britain's defeat in the American War of Independence prompts establishment of a new convict settlement.

(1783)   (John Hudson, chimney sweeper, convicted in London of theft.)

(1786)   (Captain Arthur Phillip receives his commission as governor of New South Wales.)

1788, 26 January Governor Arthur Phillip raises the British flag at Sydney Cove. The colony is officially proclaimed on 7 February. The Aboriginal population is about 300,000. The population of Greater London alone is about one million.

(1814)   (Francis Greenway, convict architect, arrives in Sydney.)

1815   Britain defeats France in the wars arising from the French Revolution, but suffers from post-war social and economic distress.

1820   George IV becomes King.

1829   In Britain, Metropolitan Police Act sets up a paid, uniformed police force in London which is later extended to country areas. The number of convictions for crime increases. During this period the sentence of capital punishment for many crimes is removed, and so more prisoners are transported instead.

(1829)   (E.G. Wakefield publishes *Letter from Sydney* in London)

1834   William IV becomes King. Point Puer established for young convicts.

(1835)   (Henry Tingley, assigned convict in Van Diemen's Land, writes to his parents in Sussex.)

1837   Victoria becomes Queen.

1840   Transportation to New South Wales ceases.

(1840-1)   (Edward John Eyre makes his arduous overland journey across the Great Australian Bight.)

(1841-6)   (Caroline Chisholm at the height of her work with female emigrants.)

1845-50   Irish famine.

1851   Opening of the Great Exhibition in the Crystal Palace, London, displaying Britain's progress. Australian gold-rushes begin.

(1856)   (Samuel Shumack emigrates from Ireland with his family. James Harding, free settler, writes to his parents from South Australia.)

1860s   Land Acts in Australia attempt to reduce the squatters' power.

(1862)   (Old Cordil meets John McDouall Stuart's exploring party.)

1868   Transportation of convicts to Western Australia ceases.

(1876)   (Tasmanian Aborigine Truganini dies.)

(1899)   (Bradshaw family goes to Alice Springs.)

1901   Edward VII becomes King. Commonwealth of Australia proclaimed.

1910   George V becomes King.

1914-18   First World War.

1922   Empire Settlement Act stimulates migration.

(1924)   (Orphans from Dr Barnardo's Homes start arriving in Australia.)

1929-34   The "Great Depression".

1936   Edward VIII becomes King and abdicates. George VI becomes King.

(1948)   (Buludja relates her life story to the author H.E. Thoneman.)

1952   Elizabeth II becomes Queen.

(1954)   (Queen Elizabeth is the first reigning British monarch to visit Australia.)

1957   "Bring Out a Briton" immigration campaign. Substantial post-war migration from European countries.

1971   Australian Aborigines send formal complaint about land rights to United Nations.

(1971)   (Neville Bonner is first Aborigine to be elected to an Australian Parliament.)

1972   Britain joins the European Economic Community.

1986   The British monarch is still monarch of Australia, but only because of his or her place in the Australian, and not the British, constitution.

1988   Bicentenary of the landing of the First Fleet.

Book List

Documents

Manning Clark (ed.), *Sources of Australian History*, Oxford University Press, 1977

F.K. Crowley (ed.), *Modern Australia in Documents, 1901-1970* (two volumes), Wren Publishing, Melbourne, 1973

Henry Reynolds (ed.) *Aborigines and Settlers, The Australian Experience 1788-1939*, Cassell (Australia), 1972

Russel Ward and John Robertson (eds.), *Such was Life: Select Documents in Australian Social History* (two volumes), Alternative Publishing Co-operative, Sydney, 1978-80

Books

Norman Bartlett, *The Gold Seekers*, Jarrolds, London, 1965

*Catherine H. and Ronald M. Berndt, *The Aboriginal Australians: The First Pioneers*, Pitman, Melbourne, 1983

Geoffrey Blainey, *The Tyranny of Distance: How Distance Shaped Australia's History*, Macmillan, Melbourne, 1968

Geoffrey Bolton, *Spoils and Spoilers. Australians Make their Environment 1788-1980*, George Allen and Unwin, Sydney 1981

*Don E. Charlwood, *The Long Farewell*, Penguin Books (Australia), 1983

Marcus Clark (ed. Stephen Murray-Smith), *His Natural Life*, Penguin, 1970 (A long novel, first published in 1870, based on real people and incidents in the convict settlement of Van Diemen's Land. For older readers. Also available in other shortened and adapted versions, such as Sue Phillips, *The Castaways of Hell's Gates*, Angus and Robertson, Sydney, 1982)

John Cobley, *Crimes of the First Fleet Convicts*, Angus and Robertson, Sydney, 1970

F.K. Crowley (ed.), *A New History of Australia*, William Heinemann, Mebourne, 1974

Ian and Tamsin Donaldson (eds.), *Seeing the First Australians*, George Allen and Unwin, Sydney, 1975.

Vivienne Rae Ellis, *Trucanini: Queen or Traitor?*, OBM Publishing Company, Hobart, 1976

*Richard Garrett, *The Search For Prosperity. Emigration from Britain 1815-1930*, Wayland Publishers, London, 1973

Mrs Aneas Gunn, *We Of the Never Never* and *The Little Black Princess*, Angus and Robertson, Sydney, 1982

Ann Howard, *Women in Australia*, Bay Books, Sydney, 1984

K.S. Inglis, *The Australian Colonists: an Exploration of Social History 1788-1870*, Melbourne University Press, 1974

Jennifer Isaacs (ed.), *Australia Dreaming: 40,000 Years of Aboriginal History*, Landsdown Press, Sydney, 1980

Nancy Keesing (ed.), *The Australian Goldfields 1851 to 1890s*, Angus and Robertson, Sydney, 1967

*Virginia Luling, *Surviving Peoples: Aborigines* Macdonald & Co (Publishers) Ltd, London, 1979

*Humphrey McQueen, *Social Sketches of Australia, 1888-1975*, Penguin, 1978

Ged Martin (ed.), *The Founding of Australia. The Argument about Australia's Origins*, Hale and Iremonger, Sydney, 1978

Brian Murphy, *Dictionary of Australian History*, McGraw-Hill, Sydney, 1982

*Daniel O'Keefe, *Australian Album – The Way We Were. Australia in Photographs, 1860-1920*, Daniel O'Keefe Pty, Ltd, Sydney, 1982

*Joe Rich, *The Australianization of John Bull*, Longman, Hawthorn, Victoria, 1974

John Ritchie, *Australia as Once We Were*, William Heinemann, Melbourne, 1975

A.G.L. Shaw, *Convicts and the Colonies: A Study of Penal Transportation from Great Britain and Ireland to Australia and other Parts of the British Empire*, Melbourne University Press, Melbourne, 1978

Geoffrey Sherington, *The Australian Experience, No. 1: Australia's Immigrants, 1788-1978*, Allen and Unwin, Sydney, 1980

Christopher Sweeney, *Transported in Place of Death: Convicts in Australia*, Macmillan, Melbourne, 1981

Computer Programme

First Fleet Data Base. Data base, teacher's handbook, worksheets. Enquiries to: Tasmania Media Centre, 252 Argyle Street, Hobart, Tasmania 7000

* indicates material suitable for younger secondary school students.

Acknowledgments

The Author and Publishers would like to thank the following for their kind permission to reproduce the illustrations: The Art Gallery of Western Australia for page 49 (top and bottom); Australian Information Service, London, for pages 10, 58 and 59; BBC Hulton Picture Library for pages 14, 15, 22, 23, 24 and 35 (bottom); Eve Buscombe for page 13 (bottom right), from Eve Buscombe, *Early Artists in Australia and Their Portraits*, Eureka Research Publishers, Sydney, 1979; Cambridge City Library (Cambridgeshire Collection) for page 34 (right); Cambridge University Library for pages 9 (bottom), 18, 35 (top) and 46; Conservation Commission of the Northern Territory (Bradshaw Collection) for page 5; Fitzwilliam Museum, Cambridge, for page 39 (bottom); Library Board of Western Australia for page 32; G.I.R. McMahon, Homerton College, Cambridge, for page 31; Mary Evans Picture Library for the frontispiece; National Library of Australia for pages 11, 26, 28, 29, 36, 37, 43 (top), 54 and 56; National Trust of South Australia for page 51; J.R. Ravensdale and Alan Russell for page 39; Robert Hale Ltd for page 41, from W.E. Harney, *Life Among the Aborigines*, Robert Hale Ltd, 1957; Royal Commonwealth Society, London, for pages 9 (top), 19, 30, 34 (left), 42 and 53; State Library of New South Wales (Dixon Galleries) for page 27; State Library of New South Wales (Mitchell Library) for pages 13 (top) and 50; State Library of Tasmania for page 13 (right); Tasmanian Museum and Art Gallery for pages 20, 43 (bottom), 44 and 45. The map on page 4 was drawn by R.F. Brien. Elaine Butt helped devise the map on page 6, which was also drawn by R.F. Brien. The Micro-Electronics Project Software Unit assisted with the pie-chart on page 57.

The Author thanks the following for information and assistance: Jim Harbison, Clem Macintyre, Ged Martin, Phyl Nicholson, Helen Pilkinton, Jack Ravensdale, John Ritchie, and those who, over the years, have known Eryldene, Sydney, and Calthorpes' House, Canberra.

Cover Illustrations

The colour photograph is from "Australian Gold Diggings", painted by Edwin Stocquelen, 1856 (*National Library of Australia*); the black and white print is "The Conciliation", by Benjamin Dutterau, 1840 (*Tasmanian Museum Art Gallery*); the figure of the convict was drawn by Nick Theato.

Index